Contents

VOICES FROM A TINCTURED HEART

A Collection of Poems

Moin Qazi

INDIA • SINGAPORE • MALAYSIA

ISBN 979-8-89186-597-6

Introduction

This book is a collection of poems written by the author over four decades and covers a diverse canvas of themes with which the author identified himself. It allowed the poet to see the world through so many lenses and opened so many new dimensions. The poems aim to inspire humanity to grasp the creative potential of those living at the bottom of the pyramid and unleash their amazing ideas to transform their world. This is the only way we can do the best for those most in need. The ultimate objective of these poems is to motivate and inspire everyone to foster a truly civilized and equitable world.

The poet is acutely sensitive to the trampling of the rights of helpless victims of injustice. He recalls in hindsight that he feels gratified he made the right decision of choosing poetry as his preferred medium of expression to plead the case of disenfranchised folks. He was able to harvest rich yields, and it helped him make so many helpless people survive and thrive. He believes that poetry has the potential to inspire great thoughts and ecstatic visions and create an indelible impact on the audience. Socrates says: "The orator speaks like a learned man, while the poet speaks the language of God."

The author reiterates that poetry is the most evocative, aesthetic, and stylistic expression that can produce a profound appeal to others' sensibilities. It is an abiding reflection of the human conscience. He believes poetry is one of those revered arts whose creators far outnumber its followers. Poetry helped the poet realise his obsession with combatting the awful inequities he saw all around. It helped him engender ingenuity and cooperation among the downtrodden so that they could solve their social problems themselves. We just need to spark their interest with deep empathy. The poet has enormous faith in the native ingenuity of the poor and feels we could become catalysts for helping them climb out of poverty and despair.

Preface

A Poet's Life

Every man is born an artist. The problem, in the words of the famous painter Pablo Picasso, "is how to remain one as one grows up." An expressive artist shapes his creative vision through a medium expressing his creative impulse. This may be poetry, painting, sculpture, music, architecture, and many other visual arts that the ingenious human mind has given birth to. Several great politicians, monarchs, scientists, and philosophers have sought the catharsis of poetry for their salvation. Einstein's and Darwin's writings have a poetic verve and such great musical resonance that it sounds like a great artist is speaking to us. Some famous catchphrases in speeches of great politicians like Lincoln, Churchill, Kennedy, Martin Luther King, and Nelson Mandela have inspired generations like no other work of art could have done.

Literature has never been my primary business. It was certainly a strange miracle that I meandered into the bushes of poetry and later used it as my strongest tool for the mission that I pursued of taking up the cause of the rights of the impoverished and bonded and subjugated women in villages. I have spent a substantial part of my life, energy, time, and career as a solitary activist because my perspective and approaches could not chime with those of my fellow men.

I was surprised to find my medium of expression very pivotal in imparting a sense of mission to the aggressiveness of my role, in a spasm of recklessness and at the same time excitement. I believed that an instinct for poetry could best be channeled as effective weaponry for my cause. I gave myself to writing about the exploitation of common folks and the life and the attendant hazards it entailed. My early success made me feel elated by the feelings that the young poet was striving for. The bohemian culture in the villages where I spent most of my life and career became the setting for the aesthetic revolution I was trying to unleash.

My poems are powered by the emotional strength of my passion for the rebellious role I was often called upon to play in life in pursuit of my mission for redress of injustice against the downtrodden. I defended the disenfranchised people against the capitalist overlords in remote areas where they commanded large swathes of land and were backed by armed supporters. My anger, which was delivered in poetic rebellion, was my solitary ally and it most often triumphed.

There are flashes of visceral imagery in my early poems that anticipate the avant-garde expansion of them in my later life. My variegated exposure to diverse causes gave me mature insights and helped me crystallize my mission and strategy. Since it took time for me to become familiar with the grammar of poetry, there are images of fragmentation and metaphysical forcefulness that stretch beyond direct comprehension.

There are contradictions in both my life and poems. Sometimes, there is a nightmarish vision of people threatening us; then there are exciting moments of success and victory against our opponents. In a similar vein, the architecture of my poems oscillates between elation and depression and is suffused with the anguish of memory and the urgency of uprising. I felt a penchant for recounting the everyday experiences with my rustic clients and friends. My life was quite complicated on account of various circumstances, including my frail health and my emotional subtleties. Hence, my life and my literary output oscillated between elatedness and depression. Many of the poems were composed in a state that has to do something with the isolation and anonymity that I experienced.

I had several conflicts with my opponents, and this is the reason why the poems do not follow a linear path. The poems synthesize and reveal the contradictions of the life I lived. This is the reason why the voice of my poems is not professionally sculpted. The poems are built on emotional symbolism and are subject to change and flux, with shifting states and necessary transitions.

My poems are usually meditations with a mordant wit that is especially sharp given its proximity to feelings of loss and despair throughout. Several elegiac poems recall death wards, hospitals, penury, acute frustrations, depression, and lives carrying on after a death in the family. The poems are less focused on rhyme scheme than on images and expression. My overall rhetoric illuminates the painful life that several people cope with when they are faced with the complexities and challenges of modern society.

I adopted a distinct self-styled structure for the poems after I found a need for a broad and sympathetic tolerance of all poetry. Those, like me, have no option but to take action on the streets to defend the livelihoods and humanity of those being oppressed by feudal overlords. The oppressors are bent on further enriching themselves and have some common cause with the anti-capitalist revolutionary who radiates a power that has grown over time.

My poems have evolved through my own perspective and are both a product of my times and, of contemporary readers. Its major rhetoric illuminates the complexities and challenges that the world is undergoing and has covered a large canvas because I am convinced that everyone should have a broad and sympathetic tolerance of all poetry.

I have enormous hope that my humble efforts, which have yielded this harvest of literary figments from a non-established and unprofessional literary soil, will inspire the audience to unleash their creativity and activism for the sake of restoring sanity, justice, and peace in this world. Poetry also has served for many as a principal instrument for both individual and collective salvation.

Chapter I

My Adventure with Poetry

I have no pretensions of being an established poet. But writing poetry has always come to me naturally. There have been moments when I found my emotions seeping through spontaneous bursts of verses. Poetry has been my constant companion and helped me face life's vicissitudes. It has been my armour and arsenal. For me, poetry is a redemptive act, an aid in finding the way back from alienation to a sense of belongingness. It has been a way of life, a journey unto a destination that I still don't know as I keep crossing one signpost after another, maturing and growing in wisdom with every new leg of my journey. I have inherited the literary DNA from my parents, who have been great patrons of Oriental literature. I was born in a family where hard work and education were paramount. I admire my parents for teaching their children the values of hard work and commitment. My father was a highly successful jurist and public figure with a vast repertoire of quotes from Oriental poetry. He taught me the values of professionalism while my mother passed on her artistic sensibilities. These legacies formed the twin strands of my genetic code. Other threads have bound us together. They taught me that life was a struggle to achieve excellence in every area one touched. My father was not so concerned with what vocation or career I chose but was keen that once I had made a choice, I must aim to excel in it.

I have been a professional banker taught and trained in the complex and coarse grammar of banking. At the same time, I am a developmental worker, always keen to empathize with people with low incomes and their causes. Working for people with low incomes became an abiding passion in the years that came, and even when I was given official assignments that had little to do with them, I would work out ways of keeping myself involved with it. The roots I had put down were not so shallow that I could pull them up as soon as my career veered into areas that could hardly nourish my creative faculties. Nor could anyone else attempt to do so. In my early days, the bank career appeared to be intellectually vegetating. I had no fascination for figures, and in the initial years, it seemed to me that banking was more a number-crunchers' delight. In later years, I found that poetic sensibilities influence one's approach to situations and play a critical role in forming a more humane worldview. They also influenced my role as a banker.

My foray into poetry was purely accidental. The muse courted me early in life, but the seduction soon faded. The early success began to blunt the poetical knife. It could partly explain my disappearance from the local poetry scene after a bold and encouraging beginning. Most of my poems are what I may call spontaneous outpourings or personal diaries that I wrote during a turbulent period of my adulthood. After churning out sentimental sludge in the early years, I settled down to disciplined writing. I later turned to journalism as I was tired of the muse. The mistress, too, deserted me, and there was a long drought. My poetry dried up because life forced me onto paths that hardly allowed my creative urges to mature and blossom. Later, when I kept itching to write poetry, it never allowed me to take the wheel. Only after almost twenty years could I tempt the muse to return.

Poetry has been my anchor. I have translated and crafted my yearnings into metaphors and motifs of poetry. I have chosen to write exclusively in English and picked bones with those who argue that the ultimate betrayal is to decide to write in a language other than one's mother tongue. I found greater clarity of expression in English because I was schooled in English, and at least half of my textbooks in college were English literature. The mechanics of poetry and how it helps in alchemizing emotions into images has been an area of constant observation and experimentation in my obsession with poetry.

The advice of Rilke in one of his letters to a young poet has been my literary compass: "No one can advise or help you - no one. There is only one thing you should do. Go into yourself. Find out the reason that commands you to write; see whether it has spread its roots into the very depths of your heart; confess to yourself whether you would have to die if you were forbidden to write. This, most of all: ask yourself in the most silent hour of your night: must I write? Dig into yourself for a deep answer. And if this answer rings out in assent, if you meet this solemn question with a strong, simple 'I must', then build your life following this necessity; your whole life, even into its humblest and most indifferent hour, must become a sign and witness to this impulse."

My individual and communal life has been through such tremendous upheavals that I would have become a wreck if my personal life did not have poetry to fall back on. Poetry was an emotional catharsis and therapeutic effect as painful memories kept dribbling out and taking indirect routes into the poetic stream. I could unspool the childhood traumas that had become embedded like demons in my mind's deep hollows and began to termite it. They became the germs for my future poems, propelling me to refine my verse and enhance its spiritual and literary qualities. Poetry has given me almost savage contentment. Whenever I found myself growing grim with life's constant worries, whenever I felt my soul warping on account of the mart of mundane economic strife and the dull aching monotony of spending consecutive days as a computer jockey and nerd, like some troglodyte, pecking out my living, I knew it was high time I must indulge in poetry-be it reading or composing or just mulling over immortal classical odes. Some of my poems may be disturbing. Some may be uplifting. Some may be shocking. I hope that, in some way, they will affect the reader. Some people keep a journal. Some write songs, some scream, and some have nervous breakdowns. I create poems to help me cope with the dizzying maze we all stumble through daily. Despite the slimness of the output and the randomness of its offerings, I still find people charmed by my plain talk. I have survived several personal misfortunes that might have crushed a lesser will and stilled a less hardy pen.

There are bitter, misanthropic and self-loathing rants, but there is also often a comic use of non sequitur, disarming frankness, surreal leaps and puns. My poems lack an incredible poise, and a calm reserve and leave adrenaline coursing down the reader's mind frenziedly.

I wasn't an excellent poetry buff in school. I dutifully memorized poems because we were supposed to, but if I were asked to recite them, they'd come out as sing-song. I didn't feel at home in the traditional English metres. At once, I warmed to the rhythms of free verse, the directness of treatment, and the clarity of the images. But I didn't begin writing poetry just then. My first attempt at creative writing was a short story called a prose poem. It was written when I was sixteen. But even then, and for some years after, I didn't realize that my poems, such as they are, would be the dominant form of my creative output. Like most people with literary interests, I thought I'd switch to fiction. I thought versifying was an exercise in handling language in a concentrated form, preparing for novel writing. Now I realize that the novel requires a different type of sensibility, a different kind of discipline. A lucky few can manage fiction and poetry; I am not one of them. An inner short-story writer is itching to break out through my stark, emaciated verse. The lines are long, the poems sputtering on, sometimes for pages, until they finally run out of gas, as if they were the first drafts of a lazy afternoon.

My poetry is earth, and I like to consciously keep that way, shunning sophistication that, while adding gloss, takes away the mystical charm from the power of verse. Poetry loses its value if it is reduced to mere versification. Metre and rhyme are essential components of good poetry but are not central. They are like the gilt edge, meant to enhance the poem's beauty and music. But the central core, the heart of the poem, is the message; how much does the news succeed in striking the deeper chords of the reader?

I frequently write about rural landscapes and the plight of the deprived and the underdogs, a combination of the poorer classes and rural life based on the environment and people around me. If I muse on the difficulties of urban life, I also invoke the hardships of village life. My poems portray the foibles of individuals that make them endearing, and the degeneration in human values is the common theme in my poetry. My principal aim in poetry is to sharpen people's sensitivity to the finer values of life, and I regard poetry as a powerful medium for promoting human brotherhood and world peace.

When I write poetry, I believe God touches me. You can take away everything from me, but you can't handle that invisible fount of the creative spirit. My sympathies are with the oppressed, the underprivileged, and those denied the right to live according to their convictions and to honour their inner light, which is the most authentic beacon for them. The mundane injustices leave an aching pain inside me. The standard and ordinary man's predicament is the focal point of my mission. For me, poetry is both a means of catharsis and a medium for highlighting the plight of the miserable. Poetry also carries a special meaning for me as exiles must sustain themselves with what they can take, their lightest but most precious burdens being memory and language. I was a compulsively inquisitive child. I was also fearful. In part, I feared myself and my roving intellect. It made me feel as if I lived apart in some cold, far galaxy of the mind. If a poem is dear, well thought out, purposive, logical and authentic, it will have changed something first in the poet himself because if it does not happen, there is no poet. I was once a journalist by profession and continue to churn out voluminous writing for newspapers. These are all parts of my praxis and make my feelings, thoughts, concerns, and full awareness of the world visible and palpable to audiences unknown to me. The only problem is the threat of it degenerating into poetic journalese.

My poetry is relatively private and spiritually engaged with issues in the secular life surrounding me. I regard my poetry as essentially autobiographical and historical. It describes my engagement with persons and places, the progression of time, death and loss, memory and perhaps a hope of liberation to which I cling. Some of my personality's ill traits have become part of the fabric of existence: some conditions must be managed daily, and no phoenix will surge renewed from the cinders and ruins of a past self. The horrors of the experience often push against aesthetics, even asking whether conventional poetic tools are appropriate in the face of shockingly lived events.

My work is steeped with the themes and travails of exile, loss, and displacement. My childhood provides the canvas for strokes from every stage of experience. Poetry makes me orient myself, express bottled-up feelings, and anchor my perception and shyness. I firmly believe everyone has the right to live according to their lights. The lights may not be the city lights-they might burn on the mountaintops or in forlorn caves-but to the person whose lights they are. They are the only authentic ones for him.

I tried to rhyme my cadences, but they appeared to lose clarity and became too turgid to ring true. I spent most of my life-fighting poverty and injustice in and around me and in the society in which I served and lived. I write poems on what I see daily and crusade relentlessly for justice for the wronged. My poems always carry the rumblings of the complex realities of life. This feeling is patent in every couplet.

My thirty-year-old career in banking and finance was suffused with several minor crusades for the right causes. My poetry is a travelogue of painful stations in my destination through a long and eventful career. It brought me close to bruised hearts and provided me with the lenses to see the deeper wounds in the tender compassion of people. I spent countless evenings in dirty slums among scores of AIDS families. The poems are a sequence of snapshots- often small, erratic and delicately imagistic - of crucial incidents in my life, moments of intellectual illumination. I have been a rebel both in my writings and personal life, always picking up quarrels, even with the best of friends.

To make my point, I quote a passage from Bernard Shaw:

> I am, and have always been, and shall now always be, a revolutionary writer because our laws make law impossible; our liberties destroy all freedom; our property is organized robbery; our morality is impudent hypocrisy; our wisdom administered by inexperienced or mall experienced dupes, our power wielded by cowards and weaklings, and our honour false in all its points. I am an enemy of the existing order.

I am blessed to have lived to inform you that even when my hours were darkest, I believed I could someday share my experiences with others. This collection is a form of struggle that keeps my spirit alive to struggle. To struggle is to strengthen my faith, hope, and belief in humanity. Since you and I exist together, we can make a difference!

Poetry demands immense commitment and concentration. As in love, everything comes out. The words tremble if they are right. As the body trembles in love, the words flutter on paper. There may be days you would keep hunkering and the poem eluding you. As the great poet Dom Moraes has written: “I worked at poetry like any apprentice at his trade. It is the hardest discipline there is, and demands more from whoever submitted to it than any other”.

While it is imperative to struggle ceaselessly against all forms of discrimination and injustice, a poet gives the heart more importance than the head and loves a more significant role in creativity than reason. In the temple of love, a poet makes his place to create a new world with new dawns and sunsets because there are worlds beyond the stars that we see. A perfect man is truthful, compassionate and fearless and one who can face death with equanimity:

Did you ask me of the marks of a man of faith?

When death comes to him, he has a smile on his lips.

Some say it's time for poets to decide the world. I'm not so sure. Things are still too slow for that. People still dream backwards for history. But everything rests forward for the future. Religions, nations, and armies: are all to the mind, and only these things slow down the world. A poet reveals what history conceals. That is why we still have a future.

Chapter 2

The Art of Poetry

Any art needs a medium (words for poetry, colours for painting, sounds for music, etc.). Everyone likely to care for art comes to learn something about the language, colour, line, etc., during school days. In this sense, they are the given elements. Associated with each medium are specific nuances. These may be motifs and metaphors or metrics and mechanics. In other words, each art has a calculus in which the art has to be moulded. We can effectively call it grammar. The grammar is well-prescribed in some cases and loosely in others. But it is always there. Then there are the tones, the colours and the texture, which give depth, meaning and resonance to the art. All artists have a common lexis in which their real passport is their art as they move through the doors of a borderless world.

Every artist is creative, but not every artist is original. The original artist takes birth in generations. Every piece of art is an aggregate of influences that have shaped an artist's vision. If every artist proclaims he aims at originality, he is pursuing something as imaginary as swamp fire, for which the Latin phrase is *ignis fatuus*. Even a great artist like Mozart has said: "I have not made the slightest effort to compose something original."

What role should an artist play in the struggle of humanity? What is his rightful place in a world afflicted by misery and strife? These questions have occurred to many artists and have been asked in Hindemith's *Mathis de Mahler*. To Mathis Grunewald, working peacefully with the Archbishop of Mainz, comes the thought that art is vanity, an escape from duty. So leaving his work, and renouncing love and patronage, Mathis joins the peasants in their resurrection. However, there is no satisfaction for him—only a sense of waste and perplexity.

At last, in a vision, he sees himself as St. Anthony and the Archbishop in the likeness of St Paul. St Paul brings him comfort and an answer to his perplexity. "Artists aren't as other men. Their special mission is divine, so return,' says St Paul, "return and paint."

The divine character of artists' works bristles in their parting words to the world. Keats said, dying, "I feel the flowers growing over me. "Byron passed on with the gentle words: "I must sleep now". Goethe called for "more light". Beethoven's most moving death phrase was "I shall hear in Heaven".

Poetry is an old and very diverse literary art form in which language is used in several ways to affect the reader. Often poems utilize language for aesthetic, evocative and stylistic reasons - in addition to the actual and material meaning and message of the poem. Poetry goes back so far into human history that it is hard to see its clear beginnings. Poetry is sometimes even argued to be a fundamental aspect of language, which works through metaphor and symbolism to create meaning. Poems have changed a lot over the ages, with specific cultures producing poetry in distinct styles relating to the language and the time and period of creation.

Poetry may predate literacy, with ancient works perhaps created to aid the oral transmission of information in prehistoric cultures. Poetry has been with us as long as the language itself. The poetic faculty is not dependent on learning; it willy-nilly finds expression like an underground spring which bursts out of the earth's bowels when pressures build up. Many of the greatest poets of the world are unlettered.

Poetry has been one of the most ancient creative channels for man. Even before the invention of the written method of communication, the oral tradition sustained man's creative output. With the birth of writing came the efflorescence of poetry. It became the vehicle of expression for all great men, philosophers, saints, savants and even kings. All great epics are beautiful specimens of poetry. As the great poet Octavio Paz says: "The relationship between man and poetry is as old as our history; it began when human beings began to be human... as long as there are people, there will be poetry". The great Greek philosopher Socrates said, "The orator speaks like a learned man, while the poet speaks like God." The Dutch philosopher Benedict Spinoza confirmed what Plato said: "The poet speaks the language of God." In the appraisal of human affairs, Shelley said, "The poet is the unacknowledged legislator of the world." Wordsworth stated that: "The poet binds by passion and knowledge the vast empire of human society as it is spread over the whole earth and overall time." And according to William Cullen Bryant, "The poet will always communicate with the distant ages."

Forty years ago, T.S. Eliot warned that a nation which ceases to produce poetry would, in the long run, stop being able to enjoy and even understand the great poetry of its past. More recently, in a lecture at Oxford, Seamus Heaney sounded a powerful wake-up call: "Poetry cannot afford to lose it is fundamentally self-delighting inventiveness, its joy in being a process of language as well as a representative of things in the world".

The finer values of human life have inspired all great poets and have a mystic strain in their message. In the famous words of Pablo Neruda, "Poetry is a deep inner calling in man; from it came liturgy, the psalms and also the content for religions. Today's social poet is still a member of the earliest order of priests. In the old days, he made his pact with the darkness, and now he must interpret the light". Neruda defines his poetry as one that "rejected nothing it could carry along in its course. It accepted passion, unravelled mystery and worked its way to the people's hearts". Louis Macneice saw poets as an antidote to slogans and fixed ideas. In the preface to his critical book Modem Poetry, he states: "The poet is a maker, not a retail trader. The writer today should be not so much the mouthpiece of a community (for then he will only tell it what it knows already) as its conscience, critical faculty, and generous instinct."

The Czech novelist Milan Kundera has said: "Indeed, if instead of seeking the poem hidden 'somewhere behind', the poet 'engages' himself in the service of a truth known from the onset (which comes forward on its own and is out in front), he has renounced the mission of poetry. And it matters little whether the preconceived truth is called revolution or dissidence... faith or atheism, whether it is more justified or less justified, a poet who serves any truth other than the truth to be discovered (which is dazzlement) is a false poet". It is our great good fortune that in the world today, there are poets who are courageously and imaginatively discovering and articulating such truths or truths for us; truths which are not already known but truths which are yet to be found; truths which can come to us through poetry, through the rhythmic action of language alone and no other medium. The insistence is on the poetic truth that is not unconnected or unconcerned with other realities but is unwilling to be a version or a follower of any different truth, reluctant to be colonised by any other fact. In this sense, poetry today is asserting its radical autonomy. Any one-dimensional coherence does not achieve the truth of poetry, but by a rich and complex inclusion: it is inclusive, it "needs no furniture", and it is defiant and undamaged by contradictions. It refuses to sum up and totalise. It restates that truth is not one but that facts are many.

Joseph Brodsky, who suffered imprisonment in Soviet Russia and later won the Nobel Prize while living in involuntary exile in the US, always privileged poetry over prose. The point is worth noting because Brodsky was a superb prose stylist, as his collection of essays, *On Grief and Reasons*, amply demonstrated. But it was poetry that was Brodsky's first love. He believed poetry lent itself to a precision more easily than prose. Moreover, literature started with poetry: "The song of a nomad predates the scribbling of a settler". Above all, he wrote, "Poetry develops in prose that appetite for metaphysics that distinguishes a work of art from mere belles letters."

A C Benson visualises the poet's role in a much broader view:

The poet, perhaps, is the man who sees the greatness of life best because he lives most in its beauty and fineness. The poet is emotional in a respectful way; he is thrilled, he loves, he worships, and he sorrows; but it is all essentially grave because he wishes to recognize the sublime and uplifted elements of life; he wishes to free himself from all discordant, absurd, fantastic, undignified contrasts, as he would extrude laughter and chatter and comfortable ease from some stately act of ceremonial worship.

Poetry is a unique possession of the Homo Sapiens, which memorably manifests and defines our essential humanity. Language is perhaps the only infinity given unto man, and poetry has survived as his inalienable mother tongue. We speak to the present, the dead, and the posterity through poetry. It invariably brings us to the neighbourhood of the other. It liberates us from the clutches of the routine, the predetermined and the predictable. It connects 'here' and 'there', the' now' and the 'eternal', the 'ephemeral' and the 'lasting': it locates us in time and space and yet takes us beyond them. It roots us in history and frees us from historical inevitability. Language dreams in poetry. It sings, questions and mediates: there is the sunlight, the darkness, the twilight of our interminable being. It renders our loneliness creative and restores selfhood to social action. When all the doors are closed on humanity, poetry, even at the risk of its existence, keeps a door open, maybe a half-open door', in the words of Tomas Transtromer, 'leading to a room for everyone'.

We are now in the twenty-first century, and despite all its disasters and mass annihilations, humanity has survived. Poetry is the most incontrovertible evidence of the human will to stay. Poetry stands by man - man is the sole objective of poetry. Not that poetry has suffered from self-doubts and crises. The totalising forces of our age have tried to ignore its voice. It has suffered suppression and marginalization. Risking being alone, poetry has stuck to its moral resolve to defend and protect man's identity, dignity and inviolability, life and language. Perhaps it could be asserted that in our time, politics, religion, science, and technology have all betrayed man and that poetry has stood by man as its permanent addressee. Man is the sole objective of poetry. We are called, therefore, to continue our lonely journey, to enter a high realm of freedom, a realm that remains limitless as long as time does not stand still and time never stands still.

The great statesman John F Kennedy considered the poet a prophet. His tribute to Robert Frost resonates with the statesman's high reverence for the poet:

And because he knew the midnight as well as the high noon and understood the ordeal and the triumph of the human spirit, he gave his age strength to overcome despair.

At the bottom, he held a deep faith in the spirit of man. And it's hardly an accident that Robert Frost coupled poetry and power, for he saw poetry as the means of saving energy from itself.

When power leads man toward arrogance, poetry reminds him of his limitations. When power narrows the areas of man's concern, poetry reminds him of the richness and diversity of his existence.

When power corrupts, poetry cleanses. Art establishes the fundamental human truths that must serve as our judgment's touchstones. The artist, faithful to his vision of reality, becomes the last champion of the individual mind and sensibility against an intrusive society and an officious state.

The great artist is thus a solitary figure. He has, as Frost said, "a lover's quarrel with the world." In pursuing his perceptions of reality, he must often sail against the currents of his time. There is a determined eagerness to charm in lines like these of Frost:

If one by one, we counted people out

For the most minor sin, it wouldn't take us long

To get so, we had no one left to live with.

For, to be social is to be forgiving.

Today, the "poetry of the world is the trustworthiness chronicle of man, his anxieties and visions, his sufferings and joys - his dreams and responsibilities. Poetry sensitizes the nether world of objects, questions the new architectures of self and imparts new sensuousness to language. In the words of Czeslaw Milosz, poetry dreams reality and "no one believes it is happening now". In a world rendered almost explicable and comprehensible, poetry surprises us with its discoveries, ever-lively sense of mystery of the universe, its attempt to restore the mysterious, rehabilitate the sacred, and reiterate the abiding reverence for all life.

Leopold Senghor rushes in, saying, "I must hide him in my intimate veins" and "break in my heart till I shed pure petals of the song". To Allen Ginsberg

Life seems like a passage between

two doors to the darkness.

The poet creates his poem while roaming in the new, warped world. Therefore, the poem has a variety of relations with the ground state world where ordinary people are busy overcoming the tensions of daily life. The poets and the familiar people are not different sets of people with other emotions and experiences. Living together in the same city (or country), they share the same experiences. An ordinary man may happen to suffer more and have more intense experience compared to that of a poet. The poet differs only because he can place his experience in a more complex landscape. This landscape is warped and contains some elements of daily life, dreams, fantasies and all those things that belong to the excited state. His world is, therefore, a different world. That is why he can easily relate two experiences (or even words), which appear poles apart and disconnected to a person living at the ground state level alone. Due to warping, these two experiences come together while on the plane of everyday life. They are far apart.

Poetry is a man's memory and a permanent museum without walls. In it, we secure much that would otherwise be destroyed or wither away. By causing language to exist where none existed before, poets, in the words of Kofi Awoonor, "look for new homes every day." The poetic voice is constantly busily synthesising: hungrily, almost anxiously, trying to relate each subject of observation to some other force, phenomenon, or abstract - to find the links between self and community, past and present, inspiration and its source, leaf and star, all folds and furrows of the microcosm.

In a world full of action, words also assume the status and dignity of action. They do not watch us from the windows and enquire customarily about our well-being. Instead, they are with us in the streets, in the homes, and the marketplaces. It is not entirely surprising that the complex plurality of the world is most contained and made manifest by words. The French Revolution aroused and disappointed Wordsworth, causing him to turn away from political ideals and seek consolation in universal nature; it made Byron a rebel but gave birth to Shelley. The chief effect of the Revolution on English life and thought is to be sought in literature rather than politics. The great wave that broke over Europe in the roar of the Napoleonic wars spent its strength in vain on the political structure of these islands, but the air was long salt with its spray. And the poems of Shelley, if it were not too fanciful to prolong the figure, are the rainbow lights seen in the broken wave.

French critic Jacques Darras writes: 'The language of poetry runs fathoms deeper than ever will the language of politics or criticism. It is the most awesome of languages to handle, as it is linked to prophesy, calling into existence what it wishes for with all its soul and body.' And here is Yeats himself: '[the poet is] more type than man, more passion than type.' There was a time when poets responded to significant, public events of their day as readily as they wrote about death or love. Milton lamented the massacre of Piedmont's Protestants, Swift mocked the new Bank of England, Byron cursed Napoleon, Whitman mourned Lincoln, and Tennyson recorded a notorious act of military incompetence in a poem" Schoolchildren once knew by heart, "The Charge of the Light Brigade". Poets, being creatures of routine, tend to settle into a style sometime in their 30s and plough those acres as if their fathers' fathers' fathers had cleared them. Read a poet's second or third book, and you will see the style of his dotage. Poets restless in their forms, unwilling to take yesterday's truth as gospel, are as rare as a blue rose; rarer still are poets like Eliot, Lowell and Geoffrey Hill, who have convincingly changed their styles midcareer.

Politics and history related to complex, exterior realities - money, machinery and people en masse. Poetry, by contrast, is inward, weightless and personal; the poet is a sensitive dreamer insulated from events and bound up with obscure questions of form. Perhaps, Shelley had sensed that public and poetic language diverged when he called poets the world's unacknowledged legislators. Nowadays, poets are not even unacknowledged commentators. Whatever happened to poetry? Once poets spoke for the age and strutted the cultural stage as stars. What would European romanticism have been without Byron or Schiller? French symbolism without Rimbaud or Baudelaire? Anglo-American modernism without Eliot or Pound?

Great occasions were marked by poems whose phrases sometimes entered the language, at least for a while. Walt Whitman's "When lilacs last in the dooryard bloomed" mourned the death of Abraham Lincoln—and Robert Frost's reading of "The Gift Outright" dignified the inauguration of John Kennedy.

All that, however, was a long time ago. Today, contemporary poetry seems more akin to collecting butterflies, painting by numbers or gazing at stars: a pleasant pursuit for enthusiasm but of little significance to anyone else. For many, the only poems that matter are advertising jingles, pop-music lyrics or rap music. Yet, to most people, song lyrics and rap remain one thing, poetry another. Whatever odd forms it may take, poetry is usually assumed to consist of words to be spoken or read independently, relished for their sound and meaning lost - valuable beyond words.

In America and Britain, two countries with great poetic traditions and equally great poetic freedom, poetry has become more than culturally marginalised: it has fallen off the map.

The beauty of a surprising image; moments of revelation or contemplation; and the pleasure of a well-turned or oft-remembered phrase are satisfactions that poetry, above all other arts, can offer. Society can afford to ignore contemporary poetry, and poets can complacently accept their isolation. But if that is how it is to be, something valuable will have been lost—helpful beyond words.

Despite all the assaults, poetry has endured in the world and will continue to illuminate our path. Poems are, to use Rilke's words, "bees of the invisible". And is one trusts, at least "a feast of brief hopes". We recall the memorable lines of Dennis Brutus: "The good smell of the dust / that is the same / everywhere around the earth". To borrow words from Nikiphoros Vrettakor, "the world is greater / and has become greater than it might contain love".

Poetry is a medium, not the end. It is only a path to reach the destination. All the pain of the poem is the pain of the poet. At the end comes both exaltation and exhaustion. Poetry is written on the ridges of the forehead. The creative efflorescence in the mind is one of those fleeting moments when the poet breaks free in a world of rapture. The completion of a poem is like a clot going out of the blood. Seamus Heaney speaks of what a poem does for its author, restoring something to the self. Good poems are not willed into being but come from things remembered with a certain aura. "It is a matter of waft rather than word choice," he tells us, with a characteristically musical turn of phrase.

Poems can also be unpredictable and unbiddable creatures. They can arrive at all hours of the day or night and woe unto the poet who is not ready to receive them. A poem is a truth-telling place and not a killing field. And what, in short, would Heaney say that poetry was good for in an age which reads so little of it? "Poetry", he tells us, "constitutes a boost to the capacity for discrimination and resistance."

If Homer obliged the gods to interfere so often in his works, it was not through devotion. He looked for surprise and was in search of new worlds. The modern poet tries to find them through images. The art of image moves us and makes us forget our habits. It obliges us to concentrate on the necessity of rebuilding everything. Of course, there is society, that same society that bears. So each poet is a revolutionist. The Chilean poet Vicente Huidobro says in his poem called 'Poetical Art':

Let them be keys, these verses.

That opens thousands of doors!

And this verse in Baudelaire's 'Correspondences':

There the man goes through forests of symbols

Hasn't it got the meaning of re-discovering the world?

The great Indian poet Jayanta Mahapatra has put it very succinctly:

But what use is a poem once the writing's done?

Words looking for what, in the dark of the soul?

Like the sound of a match striking, then over;

I know that much. When all else has failed,

The poem's words are perhaps justified.

Our reactions to the universe of men, oddities and events take different forms of expression. Artists and authors, poets and preachers, thinkers and teachers, scientists and scholars, among others, are all partners in discovering and mapping the worlds within and without. Poetry is the subtlest form of expression, and it takes birth deep within a poet due to his instinct to respond to something unusual, pleasing or unpleasant. It is a creation of powerful feelings and not a mere mechanical art. Poetry so created reveals society's most essential phases, its pregnant moments in history. It is a response to the experience of minds that have lived through the rigours of time and, to that extent, is more significant than other literary genres. The one devoted to the Russian Revolution, short enough to whet the appetite for more, is amongst the strongest in its choice of extracts and the effectiveness and immediacy of its poetry by Alexander Blok and Anna Akhmatova. The poets represented here feel the tempestuousness of the times on their pulses, and their language - its terseness, its brutal directness – brings those feelings to life with a terrible sense of conviction. But when repression has ended, interest in poetry often evaporates. Russia is the home of such poet-heroes as Mandelstam, Akhmatova, Pasternak and Brodsky; officially tolerated poets there once filled football stadiums, and people once risked their freedom, and sometimes their lives, to read something new by a forbidden hand.

Even after he passes through a lifetime of hardships and character-moulding experiences, the poet's freedom still imbues his poems with crystalline transparency, beauty and goodness. At this point, form and language - which have for countless poets proved a fatal quagmire - become unbelievably natural and appropriate, and a hitherto unseen brilliance and allure appear to lend the poems refreshing vigour. Poetry speaks the same language in war as in peace. It has the same cadence in raging tidal storms as in tranquil waters. Its beauty and resonance remain the same: the soft winter spring or the sharp autumn frost.

With its vital life force and sheer power, poetry is like prophecy. It precedes painting, music, dance, fiction and drama in announcing the advent of new eras, patterns of thought, and historical currents. Poetry is the soliloquy of that creature most sensitive to and most fiercely desirous of freedom - the poet.

A whiff of poetry may help to bring thought and emotion together for a moment. But a million machines and a billion active selves are frantically busy keeping them apart. "Reality", as Wallace Stevens has said, "is a cliché from which we escape by metaphor." The poet helps in arranging this escape. But the realities of the big machine and the big organization are no mere clichés; their presence oppresses. And even if words help to ease the pressure for a time, the leaden feeling soon returns with a vengeance.

In his reflections on the poet in our time Eugenio Montale, the Italian poet, makes much the same indictment of present-day civilization, "which believes it is walking while a conveyor belt carries it along." He explains how the so-called communication of everyday life "takes place not among true men but copies of men" and how this forces the artist either to take refuge in silence or to indulge in shameless exhibitionism, "which is inevitable at a time when action and knowledge take two different paths and meet only by chance".

Few people have the nerve to face up to the dirty little secrets from their past, which they have consigned to some dark corner of their minds. Yet they cannot always prevent memory from tripping them up and confronting them with long-forgotten events that fill them with dread like a malignant tumour. The only way they can ward off these ghosts from a guilty past is to make a clean breast of the wrongs done by them, bring out what is hidden into the open and show their true face to others.

At a time when political rag chewing, hack writing, mass media banalities and high-pressure sales talk do as much to corrupt the language as industrial wastes to pollute air and water, it is the poet's job to preserve the integrity of the written word. This means ridding whatever happens to be his native tongue of cliché phrases, stale metaphors and stock sentiments and making those who read him look at the world and into their inner life with new eyes.

According to some avant-garde critics, what the poet gives a form to is not an emotion or an idea but, in Octavio Paz's words, a verbal experience. But his choice of a particular phrase or an image invariably refers to his life. All terms have specific associations, meanings and resonances which change in different contexts in which the poet uses them. It may be that whatever he wants to express can be said only in how he arranges his words. Yet, the fact that any attempt to paraphrase it mutilates a poem does not make the question of what he is trying to say irrelevant.

W. H. Auden was the rage among young readers of new poetry in the thirties because of his bravura and dash, the note of irreverence in his voice and the fascination for many of the sediments of half-digested Marxist and Freudian ideas at the bottom of their glasses after they had drunk in long draughts the wine of his poetry. At a later stage, these dregs were often replaced by lumps taken from Kierkegaard and Niebuhr.

The early poems were easy to read, and many lines stuck like burrs in memory. They also left an impression, together with one of liveliness, of being too clever and slick. As he discarded some of his all too easily acquired beliefs and reflected more deeply on life, his work gained in density and obscurity, needing a guide to explain to the curious reader what the poet was trying to say.

What is poetry? A form of delirium? An opiate to dull the pain of living? A prayer? An incantation? A nostalgia for a lost world of innocence? A new explosive to blow up an imbecile world? A call to a change of heart and mind? It is all this and more. This is at least how the young Arthur Rimbaud looks at it when he is a sixteen-year-old boy. In his adolescence, he thinks he can use his poetry as an axe to cut the tree of knowledge at its roots and return to a state beyond good and evil. It takes him only four years to see that this is an illusion. In trying to hack the tree, he bloodies his fingers. And in striving to reach out to the Absolute, he puts his mind out of gear. In despair, he throws the axe away. He gives up writing poetry even before he is twenty.

Poetry is the only art form where the number of people creating it is far greater than the number of people appreciating it. Anyone can write a bad poem. To appreciate a good one, though, takes knowledge and commitment. As a society, we lack this knowledge and dedication. People don't possess the patience to read a poem twenty times before the sound and sense of it take hold. They aren't willing to let the words wash over them like a wave, demanding the meaning flow clearly and quickly instead. They want narrative-driven forms and stand-alone art that doesn't require understanding the larger context.

Has poetry lost its audience? Or, otherwise put, does anyone read a poem for love or in the hope of loving it? Poems are widely published. Hundreds of books of poetry appear every year. Presumably, someone reads them - poets, editors, critics, students and teachers. But are they read by ordinary people, the familiar reader?

One: poetry has yielded to the hard sciences the claim of knowing the truth of the natural world and the social sciences the privilege of elucidating the mysteries of human nature and experience.

"If the labours of men of science should ever create any material revolution, direct or indirect, in our condition, and in the impressions which we habitually receive," Wordsworth wrote, "the poet will sleep then no more than at present, but he will be ready to follow the steps of the man of science, not only in those general indirect effects, but he will be at his side, carrying sensation into the midst of the objects of the science itself." The poet turns these facts into relations and values when scientific discoveries have become familiar.

Wordsworth's formula was taken up by Arnold, who wrote about poetry as "the fortifying, and elevating, and quickening, and suggestive power, capable of wonderfully helping us relate modern science's results to our need for conduct, our need for beauty."

The outdated but ever-popular romantic image of the artist as the quintessential bohemian, wild and penniless, locked in a garret with his "muse" has almost vanished. Instead, we have the contemporary version-an assertive, media-savvy, relatively affluent, talented individual. The breed is adventurous, cheeky, fun-loving and determined to let the world become aware of its presence.

The poet bids farewell to poetry because its magic has turned out to be a mirage. He refuses to accept the values from which poetry was to provide a means of escape. He takes them only in the presence of death. He commits suicide as a poet at the age of twenty. But he ceases to be a rebel and a heretic only in his last two or three days. It was not life but death which tames him in the end. But what moves us is not the final act of submission but the first act of defiance. This enables him to increase what Starkie calls the evocative power of poetry, independently of the sense it conveys.

How right she is when she writes that "words with him are no longer intended to bear their dictionary meaning; they are no longer to express a logical content or to describe; they are a form of magic charm, they are intended to evoke a state of mind and soul. The essence of poetry does not consist in the words or the images - however beautiful these might be - poetry is the very sensation itself, and this sensation is to be allowed to find its own best expression, just as the lava stream burns out of its bed."

We who belong to a more cynical age have no right to judge harshly this poet of adolescent dreams and revolt. It is supercilious to argue that only a teenager could put so much trust in poetry and hope to cut the roots of the tree of knowledge with its aid. The point is that despite his raw youth, Rimbaud saw through the game in a few years. It has taken some of our more hard-bitten writers much longer to arrive at the same point - at which Samuel Beckett put it. There is nothing to say.

The appearance of the idea of free verse in twentieth-century Hindi poetry was a significant historical occurrence. It was directly connected with the artistic and theoretical works of the authors who published their poems in the famous anthology from 1943, Tar Saptak. The seven poets, their 110 verses and the foreword by Agyeya, where he states that the poets 'do not follow any doctrines', 'they are primarily explorers', and their poetry is not of 'an ornamental kind' - all this created a turning point in Hindi poetry, similar to the artistic revolt of the European avant-garde movements.

In this way, the literary rebellion of the seven poets was dual. It happened simultaneously on two levels: the artistic and the ideological. Both groups created a model of a writer's attitude that was supposed to be innovative and individual. This attitude inevitably led towards democracy and, consequently, the individual's freedom. From the desire for liberty originated the first and also the extreme literary and artistic postulate: a right for creative experiments, for free art. And this was the main characteristic of all the avant-garde movements.

Most importantly, they were influenced by the work of T.S. Eliot and Ezra Pound. Indian poets were fascinated by Eliot's criticism of contemporary civilization, its spiritual emptiness, decay, nihilism and loneliness; in his work, they found the means of expression suitable for their spirituality (such as irony or sneering melancholy). In Pound's poetry, they discovered innovatory language, conciseness, discipline of phrase and rhythm, intellectual ingeniousness, condensed imagery and erudition.

However, the essential characteristics of poetry, the musical resonance and the lyrical smoothness of the cadences, and the way words are strung together in chemistry remain the most enduring qualities of great poetry. The universal appeal lies in poetry that sings and responds to every man's subconscious sense of sorrow and loneliness. The finest poetry should be able to transform even a philistine heart. Poetry is designed for an era when people valued the written word and had the time and inclination to possess it in its highest form. Why do we read poetry? It is a more challenging question than it might seem. Should we view the poem primarily as a verbal construct? If so, its purpose is to satisfy our aesthetic or intellectual engagement with these words in this order. Or is it mainly an expressive act? If so, then the poem's primary purpose is to give us insight into the unique individual who created it. Is it instead a vehicle for an emotionally powerful story or image? If so, it should seek to move us and speak directly to our deepest feelings.

Plato told us that the beautiful and the good were the same but also warned us that poetry's merely imitative beauty would always delusively obscure from us the truly beautiful. Ever since Plato, poets have been torn between the impulse to make the poem a "thing of beauty" in the belief that it will therefore be "a joy forever" and the fear that poetic beauty is always "mere" beauty, a tinsel distraction from higher and more significant realities.

The last century has been tough on "beauty". Modernism's motto was "look after the truth, and the beauty will look after itself"; postmodernism thought it had seen through both Beauty and Truth as shabby imposters.

In pure and simple language, poets and poetry must be linked to the future of humanity. We grow out of touch with this great truth. We forget to accept its invitation and hospitality when our works become unspiritual and unexpressive in a quest for external success. This is what Wordsworth complained of when he said:

The world is too much with us; late and soon,

By getting and spending, we lay waste our powers.

Little we see in Nature that is ours.

The poet's thirst for freedom and avid pursuit have given poetry vitality and refreshing vigour. Poetry speaks the same language in war as in peace. It retains the same cadence in raging tidal storms as in tranquil waters. Its vocabulary has the exact stamina in the sharp autumn frost and soft winter spring unattainable by any other means, making poetry impatient with tradition, unwilling to tolerate any form of binding or control. Poetry must innovate, and therefore it is always the first to shed conventions, always the first to abandon set forms, always the first to redefine paradigms and the flag bearers of avant-garde, always the first to illustrate for us the state of unfreedom within which we exist but which the vast majority of us have never noticed or paint for us a picture of human ideals, freedoms so glorious we would never dare imagine them on our own. These comprise the two most essential forms of poetic expression, and these are what cause so many to pursue poetry, lose themselves in poetry, and worship poetry. They are also the root of so many poets' loneliness during their lives and their undying fame after they die. The siege of the poet is like the plight of a songbird whose wings have been ripped off and which keeps hurling itself against the bars of its dark cages. Poets recognise the unconscious spirit of rebellious independence in all of us and the compulsion to demonstrate that we wear no man's yoke. All great poets have held on bravely to these ideals despite the incarceration and torment they had to face for their boldness. This supreme spirit of sacrifice for upholding these eternal values is perhaps the most lasting legacy for poets and humanity. Today's poet celebrates the same confidence in his poetry.

Poems are sometimes life's only refuge of freedom for an unfree heart, perhaps an oasis of hope in the vast wilderness of a spiritual desert. One who truly understands that freedom - not only the freedom to write but also spiritual freedom in the broadest sense - which must be actively grasped will produce true poetry. The question lies not in the freedom to write; no one is reaching out a controlling hand to ground our pens. Someone has said, "We are free enough; we can write whatever we want." But are we truly free? Have we felt the lightness and freedom of birds flitting across the sky? The liberty of a cowrie shell lying in the sun on the sand? Are we so satisfied? Well, then, what more have we to write? What shall we shed our heart's blood to express? Should it not be that which depresses, oppresses one's self, which makes one feel the heaviness of one's unfreedom, be it of any kind? Does simply not being in jail make one accessible, then? This is what poetry requires one to express dearly, the tiny secrets of the innermost heart, which so many people possess but are unwilling or unable to explain. (Poets, being particularly sensitive, express them with extraordinary felicity). If one can do this, one will have readers - many readers.

Some "poets" feel they already have sufficient freedom because they have neither seen nor even imagined the space of the eagle. They are like long-caged birds that, once released, are overwhelmed and disoriented by the unaccustomed freedom, unable to use it, and even made to feel unfree. They wish to return to the cage to find the stability and security that comes with being under control. Only in the cage can they sing of their thirst for freedom and their longing for the greenery of the trees.

The great Asian poet Sir Muhammad Iqbal wrote to the equally accomplished German philosopher saying that their intellectual attainments could not be put to the test of comparison as Goethe lived and breathed in a free kingdom while Iqbal wrote in a country where people were bonded with the imperial yoke of the British.

Poetry is before we think about it. Poetry comes before thought. We live in poetry, and poetry lives in us without our thinking about it, just as a tree lives by air, sun and water without thinking about it. As nature and the universe belong to those who read its mysteries, poetry belongs to those who read it. This is to say that nature is a giant womb swarming with seeds and embryos, and poetry, too, is a womb and seed ball in which we are born anew. All language is a ball of roots, but especially so is the language of poetry. We are moved by poetry, and our feelings and consciousness are expanded by poetry as if we were pregnant - this indicates that the space of poetry is pregnant and ready to give new birth to us. Poetry is the matrix of a new being. It was so in time immemorial, and it is so today. The desire to be born a new is one of the strongest desires of humanity. This is the dream so long as we desire this life to be worth living and this world to be worth living in.

Poets write to bring others a meaningful perception of life and events. They seek to widen and sharpen contact with their area of existence, to interpret, to share with others the expression of what so often seems inexpressible: the experience of being mortal and the consciousness of this human condition unique in each poet's voice but universal to all. They are on the side of angels, they are crusaders, and they carry their crusades in as many languages as they can write. Even after he passes through a lifetime of hardships and character-moulding experiences, the poet's freedom still imbues his poems with crystalline transparency, beauty and goodness. At this point, form and language - which have for countless poets proved a fatal quagmire - become unbelievably natural and appropriate, and a hitherto unseen brilliance and allure appear to lend the poems grace and rhythm.

With its vital life force and sheer power, poetry is like prophecy. It precedes painting, music, dance, fiction and drama in announcing the advent of new eras, patterns of thought, and historical currents. Poetry is the soliloquy of that creature most sensitive to and most fiercely desirous of freedom - the poet.

The poet's thirst for freedom and avid pursuit have given poetry vitality and refreshing vigour. Poetry speaks the same language in war as in peace; it retains the same cadence raging tidal storms as in tranquil waters, and its language has the exact stamina in the sharp autumn frost and soft winter spring unattainable by any other means, making poetry impatient with tradition, unwilling to tolerate any form of binding or control. Poetry must innovate, and therefore it is always the first to shed conventions, always the first to abandon set forms, always the first to redefine paradigms and the flag bearers of avant-garde, always the first to illustrate for us the state of unfreedom within which we exist but which the vast majority of us have never noticed or paint for us a picture of human ideals, freedoms so glorious we would never dare imagine them on our own. These comprise the two most essential forms of poetic expression, and these are what cause so many to pursue poetry, lose themselves in poetry, and worship poetry. They are also the root of so many poets' loneliness during their lives, and their undying fame alters their deaths.

Good Pope John once told the editors of Readers Digest while extolling their crusading spirit: "How comforting it will be for you when you come to the close of your lives on earth, to be able to say to yourselves: We have served the truth." It is to poetry that we turn when life waylays us with losses or with gains, with moments of joy or with great disaster. This has been true since language began. From prehistoric times through all recorded times, human beings have sought to make sense of their lives and the lives of others to deepen their understanding of what it means to be alive.

The dream is motion and action. Poetry is the art, the spell, of invoking the beloved, bridging his absence, and building a road between being and non-being. The dream of poetry has given birth to breathe, which in turn blows into the spirit of the man who hears the poet; this breath of imagination invites him to participate in the process of embodiment, the incarnation. If we think about it, this is the process of sharing in the passion of absence, but when we are with poetry, we feel the pain of individuation disappear, and joy swells up in this sharing. This is precisely the meaning of music and dance Nietzsche tried to share with us.

Lack is suffering, fullness, and joy. Life and history give us pain because of absence, but this lack is that which makes dreams - makes songs. This is where the greatness of the song comes in. We are poor, but our music need not be lacking. Our theme may be about sorrow, but it satisfies the dream of suffering and gives us the peace of fulfilled joy as long as it remains a song. Paul Reverdy has said that poetry does not reside in things, "otherwise everyone would easily find it, as everyone so easily finds wood in the tree and water in the river" and that a thing can become poetry only with the help of words.

When Rene Char says, "The orchid burns in the soil, " he means that the fire which nourishes the flower at the top of a long stem is derived from the earth. What is true of a flower is also true of a work of art. However high it may soar, it is in the mire of the poet's experience that it finds its nourishment.

There is hardly a poet who has not written of the transforming power of imagination - "the power by which one image or feeling is made to modify many others", as Coleridge puts it, "and by a sort of fusion to force many into one". His special gift lies in seeing relationships between things and feelings and thoughts where others cannot see any and in giving these relationships a unity or form, which takes us by surprise. He cannot do so if he is not in love with language because it is his power over words which enables him to fuse his experiences.

The best lyric poems - think of Keats or Shelley, for example - are moments of epiphany, a sudden opening onto magic casements. And Darwin, throughout, was in the grip of something very similar: a terrible, destabilising sense of wonder. He sensed intimations of the marvellous everywhere he looked. All the sadder than that, later in life, the man who carried with him on the Beagle a copy of Milton's "Paradise Lost" found that he could no longer enjoy poetry.

Chapter 3

A Collage of My Poems

01. Creating A Poem

I sit confused at my table. The mind ablaze
With visions that keep thronging it.
Teasing, disparate images floating about.
It's like a dragonfly in a dream -
Darting here, there and about
But never within my grasp and reach.
Frustrating me to the point of turning me crazy.
I want to morph these images into words
Before they vaporize and ride out of my mind.
A melody of trembling peace haunts me
But the thoughts blaze for want of real fire.

The phrases soon start sprouting and taking root.

I have to slice and peal the ugly idioms

To let the true moat of emotion float free.

I want to cultivate the consummate poem

Before reason can mangle the celestial visions.

Poetry cannot strike roots in a Fallow palm.

A whole phalanx of actions must converge

To sieve visionary impulses from the mad frenzy.

I draw my nourishment not from my roots

But from the desert of my rootlessness.

The philosophical streams have converged and

Incubated in my subterranean mind.

As they get slimed by their saliva,

Emotions and passions get frozen in time

Then melt, hibernate, churn and get seeded.

Their alchemy weaves the threads of harmony

Into the warp and weft of poesy's loom.

The words keep gushing through

In a perennial waterfall

As the wheel clatters along.

Notes succeeding notes

As if driven by the force of gravity.

Till the defining word cuts through

The bonfire of pulsing phrases.

The doors of visions start opening

One pathway leads into the other

As each deep opens into another deep.

A primal celestial force sets my

Constipated thoughts spinning free.

I have some dim intuition of a poem.

In my breast are locked visions

Aching to burst into idioms.

There comes a time when, after

With much suffering, the tree must bear fruit.

Incidents in life that seemed disjointed,

Like so many scattered leaves

Swept by the heedless winds of fate,
Seem to fall into an ordered pattern.
I couldn't have strung these words together.
The way they chemically react with one another,
A rare alchemy transmutes the visions into verses
As the ink captures the writing in the eyes,
The unquiet soul takes wings:
I know that now I am going to write.
The silences have congealed into stiffened words.
On my flight, the breast is filled with poetry
Yielding a fistful of verses.
Do you expect these lines to come easily?
Or be chaste! This isn't prose.
I've burned my best words in poetry.
From inner combustion comes a prophetic vision
And the soul, hungering for divinity, starts
Seeing the celestial outposts.
It is as if I have melted my flesh.

I have unfurled all my unspent passions
In blood into luminous cadences.
Can anyone drain my life out?
Am I not the one who lives in words?
The letters that inflame my spirit
Keep growing before my tired eyes
And in the myriad poems lives the essence of my soul
My soul has been grained from a thousand pains
And poetry dredged from deep crannies of the brain.
I have seen the world through a jeweller's loop.
After all the pain and ache that has drained me
What permeates the heart is an angelic glow.
It is like the stubborn clot-dissolving away
The blood freely coursing down the veins.
Yet, the sweetest lines are those
That still didn't come through.
The lost poem still sleeping in my weary eyes.

02. Transformation

She was eyed by everyone
As the swooning beauty rode
Sprightly through the corridors.
Walking with the gait of a queen
She looked like an empress in waiting
Her narcissi eyes were made from
The smile of light
But, did you see her now?
She sits now on the hobbling seat of a torn marriage
With broken pride and shameful humility.
She has slid from the pedestal of sanity
As she slinks past the hostile inmates.
People say eyes are a portal to the soul.
Her eyes have hollowed out of tearing grief.
They keep smouldering like lanterns.
Yesterday the beauty was chosen

To glorify a home, adorn a family tree.
Today she is being shunned as an Epigone.
Her lambent world has grown cold.
She lives like an interloper, hounded like a heretic,
Sorrow has stopped her fluorescent eyes.
Yes, she is now a stranger in her own home:
But why this tragic metamorphosis?
Dissensions rocked her inchoate marital ride.
She came to a home
That didn't accept her as a bride.
She became a quiescent slave
Crouching at the edge and
Plugging away for the breadcrumbs
Of family approval for every need.
Slinking into the narrow fortress of her room
At the wild rage of the matriarchs of the house.
She was married to a boy

Who didn't accept her as a wife?

As she cowered under

The drone of the waspish crones

She became a hostage in the very house

She came to adorn as the reigning deity.

03. Messenger of Kindness

He lightly wore people's sorrow

In cafes, in parks and public.

His heart was a castle of love, the intensity of love

As wide as the open sky,

Its sluices and levees always wide open to allow

Love's torrent to flow in easy streams.

Like a goblet that pours out its contents

Emptying himself for others was his pleasure

Everyone's problems would swim into his ken.

He thought himself into love

And dreamt himself out of it.

His architecture was one of sadness.

But if you scratched his tender frame

You could always find love lurking inside.

A constant angel pulsed in his boundless heart.

His joy was pure as rain and green as grass.

He would always creep one mile uphill
To light candles in deserts of darkness.
His acts levitated him beyond his peers
Imposing a superior moral will
Upon the dross of everyday life.
His fabled heart was torn within,
He concealed the wrench with a smile
But later went into a silent sulk.
His tolerance had reached an apogee.
It was not a onetime severance of limb
But an oozing wound that won't heal.
It became a cracked pitcher
With life slowly seeping out.
The fire that lit others' lives
Had grown too cold to hold him.
His heart became a candle
Nibbling at its soot.
He sloshed down his pain at the taverns

Baring his heart to the bartenders.

The remorse was too harsh and flaming.

It was not a banker's heart he carried

It was the poet's cavort, soft, tender and fragile.

The sorrow finally engulfed his heart

Till his eventual descent into insanity.

A worn edict of a smile cut out on his face

A final postscript to his loss and delusion.

The poetry, alas, had folded wings.

A prophet forever snuffed out. His corpse

The final relic in a saga is now laid to rest.

04. Search For Self

When will I find the real me?

I search myself in worded portraits

That people have painted of me.

My silence is construed as arrogance,

My hermitage living as snobbery.

As if I am a mandarin from another planet;

A survivor from a vanishing tribe;

A unique denizen retrieved from a hoary civilization.

My universe was never able to connect with theirs,

An incorrigible social geek pursuing a vain chimaera.

My speech too spouts raw primal feelings.

My shyness has reinforced this image:

The averted gaze, the hunched shoulders,

The body pivoted away from the crowd

As I keep shrinking away from people.

People have no ear for my words

They don't want my words to be mine
I am a misspelling chalked on the slate of time.
Yes, I am a fruit that has ripened much before time
I rode into manhood while still an adult.
All this has lent me weariness beyond my years,
I have become a tomb to my living corpse
And lost my being in so many beings.
Because my face is broad with smiles
The sunshine on my forehead betrays
The deep soulful stirrings in my heart.
I have held my aching pain for so long.
Nobody knows my secret griefs and aches
Because my face is broad with smiles
And my heart keeps longing for others.
What evil influence ruled my birth I don't know
What malignant star got stuck in my firmament?
My august pedigree has chained me

As I pursue the lost Grail of holy truth.
I sit emptying hours
And then gathering them again
As I survey my kingdom of pains.
I wander endlessly in my inner wilderness
As if all the grief comes to roost here. I feel
A messenger of sorrow that descends from the sky
Seeks out my address in this vast universe
And then the address lives forever.
I have spent my life reaping evils I have not sown.
My life has dragged its long weary way
Through years of tormenting grief.

I follow the sage advice of my school teacher:
The best way to handle a foe is to make him a friend
Even if your heart does not vibe, keep smiling
And keep shaking hands as you counter them.
I am now trying to fashion a new core

For myself, late though in life.

I want to chart out my *furrow*.

People find life in the shape of happiness,

For me, it is a shadow that keeps bolting

Like horses. Keeping behind the broken hooves.

I am a struggling plant uprooted from its soil

That has not been able to find roots again.

I am a prison where I am both the inmate and jailor.

I have come from far away, but still have a long way to go.

I am a traveller relentlessly pursuing a vain signpost.

It is like a mirage that keeps receding

Like a tree's shadow in the car's windscreen

Until it becomes a distant fading dream.

Iqbal's immortal lines keep resonating in my mind:

Do not measure this in the hour-glass of time

Of yesterdays and the morrows to come.

I seek solace in the wisdom of the Pope:

"Act well your part, there all the honour lies"

This land of dragons will soon crumble to dust.

A new world will emerge from its ashen clay.

05. My Father

Doing work.

Caring for children

Preaching good values.

He wasn't a conventional preacher

With vapid moralizing and

A hostage to nostrums and ideologies.

The flame glittered before him,

But he fought the insidious cold with fingernails.

He had a festival of stars

Laid bare at his feet

And the moon embedded in the hooding eyes.

I was his lone footsoldier

Struggling to live up

To his sanctimonious ideals,

Courting people I didn't agree with.

In every battle he fought

I was his shield, his intrepid soul shadow, his mascot.
I was virtually lab-manufactured for the task.
His will governs the essential patterns of our life.
We held him in reverential awe.
His stern advice was a pithy one-liner:
Work for your soul's sake,
That all the clay of you, all of the dross of you
May yield to the fire of you,
Till there is nothing but light!
Nothing but the light!
His quiet voice of reason
Made the world look noisy and mad.
He released an ardency that couldn't die.
His face looked serene, calm, sage-like,
The forehead ridged with crevices of wisdom
Even when sorrow grazed his heart.
There was a demon of energy at work within him
He always revelled in the challenges of life,

His life was a story of growth from humble moorings
To all the vast dreams realized ethically.
His conduct was chaste as a knife.
He had two avatars in his disposition:
One, an irascible temper; the other, a Sufi smile.
One could inhere seamlessly into the other.
His rapier wit and sardonic humour
Hit people in the solar plexus. It
Would always tickle a funny bone
And make everyone chuckle at every turn
Wondering where the visceral ended
And the cerebral took over.
He would pass like a meteor
Stirring us to a sense of higher living.
He had his eclectic brand of spiritualism
Fired by the visions gleaned from venerable Sufis
And tempered by the wisdom
Distilled from his professional life.

The words evoking the power of a preacher
And not that of an infantry on the prowl.
He was a blue chip stock on the orators' bourse.
His faith had no place for spiritual inertia.
To me, he looked like a knight in quest of a Grail.
I have inherited his large head and the wisdom
Distilled from nights of burning midnight lamps.
He couldn't hold the truth from exploding out;
The hubris would get their right desserts.
So strong was his sense of justice
That no bias could blight his judgment.
He couldn't help sermonizing to visitors
Even if they didn't have an appetite for his soul stuff.
He was thrifty of time and for knowledge seekers
He would condense an ocean into a pitcher.
His diary was flooded with gnomic entries
Which he unfurled at his small gatherings.

Like the roll of temple bells on the forehead

They were uplifting and elevating.

He untied the mental knots like a consummate philosopher.

His discourses were an intellectual emetic

To cleanse mental singeing.

Like a glow-worm at night he would illumine

The dark and misty nooks in the minds of his visitors.

He knew he would continue to shine

In the afterlife which history would grant him.

Despite his great deeds his sharp temper

Never allowed him to become a folk hero.

His words, like swords, had sharp metal,

Prising out hidden conspiracies from their minds.

At the law courts, it would be a verbal sparring of

One scissor-sharp brain with another.

He was a superhuman legal gladiator

Crunching through the arguments of opponents.

He would cut sharply through the clutter
And put the finger on the hub of the argument.
This nature would follow him at home too.
He would often play mental solitaire with me.
He wouldn't mince words, calling a spade a spade.
His eloquence and erudition as a raconteur
Shone through his deftly calibrated words.
His thoughts had the clarity of filtered light.
He would explore new contours on an old map
Taking chances in new uncharted topographies.
He forsook the mean streets of hypocrisy
For the exalted road of righteousness.
He sought in the modern corrupted age
The heroism and moral purity of an age gone by.
He wanted to clone us in his cultural mould
Like robotic animals in a menagerie.
He would often recite Iqbal's couplet:
If from his father's learning, a son takes no light,

Over his sire's legacy, how can he stake his right?
His moral purity was a talisman for his siblings.
We were passive messengers of his doctrines.
Maybe the servile obedience has hardened so much
That we have long lost our adaptive instincts
And could never match the daring of our peers.
His strict regimen would keep our synapses on edge
For his friends, he was a litmus paper
With which they tested their integrity.
His radar blipped imperceptibly at such encounters
He showed puck-like instinct in public life
And a judge-like rectitude in my personal life,
These were the only arsenals in his crusade.
He was a lone upright tree in a barn of turncoats
He was a solitary guest at his spiritual sanctuary.
He had lately chastened his tempers and mellowed,
The embers lose their cruel redness to grey ash.
Fruits sweeten when they ripen;

Old age is one such fruit.
We summoned the courage to tell him:
It is long since you have been pensioned off
Father, it is time to rest now
To close your eyes on the world.
Leave the worries to the young.
The world is too difficult now.
Our wisdom didn't go unheeded
And like a wizened sage
He deferentially honoured our humble advice.
His face had come to belong
To a world which had become silent.
Too uncivilized for his refined manners.
He watched the approach of twilight:
It was now the autumn of his life.
The springs of life had dried up.
I could see his pace slacken.
The zeal had faded

The fair was almost over:

He bowed before the altars of wisdom.

Death came unannounced to him,

Life suddenly snapped like a dry twig.

06. Cleanliness

They talk in innocent tones
Of cleanliness and hygiene.
They frown at others
Who eats on pavements,
And then expatiate
On the theories of bacteriology.
But look at their homes!
Their servants wreathed in shaggy rags
With dirt hanging like lichens
Oozing putrid odour
From bacteria-infested bodies,
Their skin sheathed in coats of stench
Their bodies glisten with beads of sweat,
They cook with their hands
That harbour microbes
Hanging in scores

Under their nails.

These are the people

Who makes a fad of cleanliness?

07. The Night

Minutes hang across the roof of time.
Time hangs limp as
Every second trickles slowly
On the palm of measurement.
We must rush to the destination
For fate shall bridle our passions
And young couples
May flaunt their happiness
To besiege our hearts.
The day passes, evening falls,
As stars unfurl over the sky
The horizon is swallowed up by
The last glow of the vermilion sun.
The earth begins to shift from its axis.
The soot-faced clouds frown and bellow,
The ghosts of the town trail in the sky

As the stars grow tired and dim.
The world has grown alien,
I have to endure the tedium of a protracted night
As its mantle keeps growing. I am awake
Awaiting the unknown angel at the door.
The night moves gingerly through the space of time.
It has still not cleared its throat and stands limp.
Who could break the stonehold of the night?
It seems night would mutate into a dreadful dawn
As it keeps spewing a strange odour.
The sequined constellation is the only soothing balm
Until the sun starts shaking the reeds of the night.
And haplessness fences itself on the path to glory.

08. The Labourer

We watch the labourers
Work in cauterising light
And sweat their brows
With overbearing fatigue.
From sunrise to sundown
They struggle in the field
For a solace-livelihood,
And a consolation for the family
But we, the pitiless masters,
Not realizing the wretchedness
Give words of encouragement,
A banana and a cup of tea
Which we expect to work as heroin.
And they, the victims of innocence,
Work with backs to the wall
For a weathered ten-rupee note
Just enough for a half-meal.

09. The Sun Shall Rise Again

The wind rustled slowly

Past my indolent limbs

As I groped in my dark caves.

My limbs tingled in fear.

In the dark someone paced

The chambers of my life.

I heard the footsteps:

A voice wheedled its way into my ear.

Like a worm

On a nocturnal prowl.

Slow, soft and stealthy steps

Echoing in the wilderness.

In the stark chambers of my heart

I heard him.

I didn't see him.

I couldn't. I heard him

Pacing like a prisoner

In a charmed cave.

A foreign piece carved out by sleep.

An unclassified gleam, a person I've

Never met inhabiting my eyes.

The silence was heavy,

It glided like rusty darkness

Over my being.

All was quiet around me

Except within my heart.

I screamed, and the words were scattered

Like a handful of germinating seeds.

They fell and were lost in the ground.

Maybe if nature is kind they will sprout.

Life is a procession of reveries,

Of memories, fraying, manuring into nightmares

Or getting recycled into blissful dreams.

The sediments of churning memories stare.

They keep colouring my sleep.

A sort of dirge rises in my heart,
A kind of pain shoots in my frazzled brain.
It starts beating and bleating like an engine;
A vague wilderness pervades it.
I must wring out the last secret from it.
Memories plough my blistered dreams
With an oblique suckling of the nerve,
Imprisoned in the labyrinths of my mind
That is searing up the filaments of my memories.
They have lost their bearings.
My mind has become a surging quagmire, where
They hibernate, breed and plop out unannounced
Sailing in a stealthy procession, they
Dog around, mocking the tethered gait.
Maybe I need a lariat to pin them down.
The embittered years seem to be
Sewn and etched firm in the mind,
The brain does not seem to be helping;

It takes off and then thumbs its nose.
I have to keep it always hooked to a task
To prevent it from going off track.
It defies logic and reason,
It takes you on a trip of time and space
And weakens your resolve.
I keep shadowboxing with Freud's ghost.
I have been stirred by strange fits of passion,
I feel as if cerebral ants are mining my skull,
I want to excavate deep within myself
In the alleyways of the subterranean world.
I want to meet the various versions of
My former me with new enlightened eyes
To confront the demon of dementia.
A trip into paranoia will at least clear the air.
I fear no ghosts, I dread no angels.
Yet wilderness is where souls are vulnerable.
My feet are chained; and the wrangled limbs

Have withered and grown callused
Like the roots of an aged magnolia.
I squirm in my bed, consumed by an oppressive fever.
My lungs burn, my heart sears wildly,
Time hangs limp. My temples roar;
The night rolls in my eyes
As I suck at the paps of darkness.
The birdsong courses through the stillness of the morn
And the sun's gold glance wishes me good morning.
The night has chomped more than its share of hours.
Far away the temple bells peal in symphony,
The cadences of the muezzin's call
Slice through the misty air.
There goes the night
As the stars start growing pale.
Here comes the morning with its shining scalpel
To open the unhealed stitches of memories.

The sun rises, so shall His light
Returning always from its slumber
To light the path out of sorrow.
Grace transcends night, offering hope, once again
Beyond adversity.
Beyond the edge of disparity,
But the azure blue is soon invaded
By the ambering refraction of the sun.
I long for the day
When I could cut the memories
And drain the muck
Out of the blackened entrails
To let my mind be purged
Of the malignancy
That keeps festering now and then.
I have lost my mind:
Lord, take me back to my time
And put an end to this unending blight.

10. Through The Hidden Eyes

The pages of my life
Eddy in the air. Like autumn leaves.
They unfurl
The unhappy events
Of my childhood.
The circlet of memories keeps floating
Unable to find a watery grave.
Those bitter memories
That has stuck to the soul
Keep my subconscious constantly awake.
No drug can jettison them from the mind
Nor can ECT warm them into vapours.
The drugs have tinkered with too much
With the synapses of the brain,
Maudlin dreams refuse to dissipate;
If only I had a hideous crucible

I would have decanted these dreams
Or by simply pressing 'delete'
I would have had them effaced.
Or with a mental sieve
Could have filtered the unpleasant ones.
Or through hypnosis
Purged them from the mind -
They have frozen too hard
To disperse now with barbiturates.
They dope me with toxic drugs
But it gives me only a transient peace.
Perhaps if somebody can tamp the womb
And blow out the hydras, it should help.
Every night I need to masticate my mind
To cleanse it of the festering emotions.
My heart was once a fortress of fortitude
But now anxiety, which could not bite
Even through the thick blanket of

Depression has begun to maul and chew.

I am like wood that depression has wormed like termites

It has cropped my soul with its swooping scythe.

It continues to lay siege to my mind.

I could once slap down these demons,

Now they have grown larger than life.

Those distant happenings

Had once been concealed

In the dark attics of my mind.

But now the gale

Has shaken the cobweb. And they have flown

And fluttered afar.

11. The memory trap

The maze of memories

Has trapped me

In its trenches.

It will not allow

A safe passage for

My new self to emerge.

There are moments

When I look back

And see the deserted road

Chasing me.

The night runs to an end

With the madly chiming clock.

Do I pick up some pebbles?

From the sediments of the night

Or leave the shore empty-handed

Like the lost, forlorn fisherman?

12. Episodes Of Childhood

How can I close
The much-discussed episodes
Of my misdoings.
Or repaint
The black words
In silver.
My life is not a golden chapter
Written in blithesome words
With silver couched pens.
It was a miasma of mental wretchedness
That closeted me
In dreams and actions.
My mind is gagged by grimy scraps of betrayals
My soul is in deep torment,
The turmoil aching to escape its mortal coil,
My world contracting into a bolus of anguish.
Father, you console in high-sounding homilies,

You make it sound so simple,

As if with the blink of an eye

I can erase those smouldering 50 years.

Isn't that how you see it?

The memories of pain won't fade so easily.

Father, you can never know

The anguish that smote my heart.

My bruised and shattered heart

Will not instantly be pieced together.

You don't know how many tribulations

You have laid at my feet.

A meteor of hope can't burn all my blues to ash.

How can hibiscus hold its ooze red when

The roots are desiccating into gnarls

And the garden retracting its promises.

All the deeds I lay under

Your barefoot

That I may find my measured grave.

13. Liberation

I have concealed myself
In so many disloyal minds.
The memories I should have kept
A closely guarded secret
Have disinterred and
Become common knowledge.
If I break open the door
The images skimp out
Like flapping butterflies.
My innermost self
Has been revealed unreservedly.
I want to blow the dust off my past,
I want to forget the chains from the past
Bind me. But how can I expunge
The memories recorded in family albums
Or narrated in anecdotes swapped between friends?

Their gossip mill keeps my past awake.
Sifting through the tree leaves of personal lives
Seems to have become a favourite sport.
Darkness has such a complex fragrance:
It evokes an involuntary flood of memories,
It opens the congealed fist of the past.
The stories begin to ripple out
As if the olfactory cortex of the brain
Has roused the rest of the house.
My heart has grown weary hearted
Like the hollow waning moon shorn of its gleam.
Memories don't shed leaves like trees in autumn,
Here they have lost their sap, dried and fossilized
But find rebirth in a different form.
Every time I enter and coffin them
They resurrect, getting a fresh lease every time.
The runnel of memories coalesces again.
Time is the great nourisher of these broken remnants,

They keep emerging out of the shroud.
They swoop on me with renewed vigour.
I am trying to peacefully part from the past.
I want to end the standoff that began with life long ago.
Father, how can I walk ahead?
The path is long and weary;
It stretches like a dreadful shadow
And they have strewn it with thorns.
Fear, the rhinestone-eyed monster,
Guards the passage.
The doting mother wants me
To take my feet back.
A shiver runs down my spine.
Father, how can
I walk ahead?
I want to escape the evil eyes
And withdraw into monastic exile

That can give peace, serenity, and freedom.
Like Siddhartha, I can't slip away at midnight
Leaving behind my wife and children.
I yearn for the day when the night
Will wrap me gently in her sable sheet
And with a leaden sigh, thou wilt invite me
To rest my aching body and weary brain.
I am trying to tame these darker promptings
And channel them into poetry.
From the dawn of my life, I have been
Waiting for my life to turn a greener leaf.
When will I get a final reprieve from this world?
I wait impatiently for the hour of final amnesty.

14. Hallucination

Dark is nearer to my heart than light.
When the light fails and you are surrounded
By darkness, do not despair, take heart -
For a thousand million stars must die each night
Just so that a new dawn can emerge tomorrow.
Where I am cannot be found on any map
That any man or machine can replicate.
The page has been wormed off the atlas
And the geography redrawn.
I am the yearning of the possessed.
I am the brutal dream of the oppressed.
If you are searching me for a meeting, then
The right place to acquaint me is in my poetry.
My family tree has grown into a dense topography.
You will be lost in the maze of its wilderness.
Vacant darkness has filled my heart,

Nameless forebodings meander in.

The long window looks down

On a dirty courtyard, and poor folks,

On their nightly foraging prowl,

Call across or scream across or walk across

Defying physics in the stream of their will.

The voices rise through several octaves.

Once in a while

When reason takes a holiday

Flippant fancies rattle like bones without ligaments

Building faerie palaces in the air.

They blow softly around my weary head

Colliding, breaking,

Engendering acute pain.

When you seek tangible solutions

They appear like foam dregs

Left by a receding wave.

The mind's squishy balloon soars to clouds

Only to squash and plunge into the depths.

These frail splinters keep the coarse blood glowing

Salvaging brief asylums from a mind-washed clean of bliss.

In the quiet testimony of my enlightened eyes

The mind hovers around the wounds.

The soul sizzles with thirst

As I scour the mind's desertscape.

All around me, there is restlessness.

The wind wreathes violently around me.

Images rise of their volition

On tiny spider-like legs

And crawl across my vision.

I have no anchor; I am drifting all the time.

Life never stops testing me,

I have been moored and unmoored several times.

Adrift on a raft without a destination

Gloom stalks in the backyard of my cottage.
In front, the sky was seared by the ambered sun,
Silence brooding in the backwaters.
The old man passed across in my reverie,
Crinkles sitting on his cheeks
And the skin cracked into scales
Like clay models crumbling under the sun.
I wish I could fly like a pair of doves -
Two handfuls of prayer raised heavenwards.

15. Chasing The Rainbow

The morning of every chapter
Hardly shows
The torment and distress
That sticks below every page.
But as evening straddles the large canvas
Every page seems
To have a philosophy.
The morning hardly shows
The anguish
Lying in store for the evening.
The evening shows
The lack of wisdom
And barrenness of sagacity
Of the morning hour.
When the moon arrives
The sun must fade.

Lord, give me any trial
But not the emptiness of evening
When hovering vultures lick the wounds,
And there is no sign of morning
To dry the festering sores.
The craters of the eyes
Pour tears in incessant bursts,
My identity lies gaping like a wound
Unrecognized, untended, unwelcome.
Noises rise and are lost in air like balloons,
The wind is a thorn in the flesh of the night
And moans aloud like a witch in the fire.
Darkness has captured my fears.
In times of family reunions
I experience extremes of loneliness
And thrash about in the labouring night
Till I am subsumed in its morbid waves.
I am an idea meant to allow

Other ideas come into play.

My Lord, my Lord,

Why hast thou forsaken me?

I do not need heaven in my grasp,

All I am used to is this beautiful earth.

16. The Alchemy Of Years

A procession of memories rolls along
As I sit with a vacant mind.
The dry weeds burn within,
Fanned by doubts and fears
Into a silhouette of distraught images.
In the ashes, the memories germinate
And then sprout into weird visions.
The video of the past is screened again
Taking me back down the vista of years
As my mind spins with hoarded memories
And begins to move in a vertiginous trance
With horror trances that have robbed me
Of precious time, of priceless grey matter.
I try to retrieve the loss with the colours of
The fading silver memories
But soon the charm wears out.

I now lead a minimalist life.

As I find it is anguish all over again

My past has slipped away like loose change.

There are sudden bursts of joy

But these are all temporary surges

That fades as surprisingly as they emerge

And drive me into a whoosh of defeat,

Rustling the barometer of my moods.

The matrix of my life has become highly volatile

The earth has been a prison to me all my life.

I want to blow the dust off my painful past,

I want to uncover the great pain

My mind has to constantly wear

And fill the crevices in the broken slate of childhood

With the glue of glutinous poppies.

I am at a crossroads:

The silhouette of the past looms large

To foil the glare of tomorrow.

17. A New Dawn

A new dawn sweeps in like a tidal wave

And in the current I am swept up like a constellation of cries.

Tossed up like flotsam by the surging passions

With my startled eyes

White in a skyless season

Even when I am happy,

A sliver of pain always works

It's way into my consciousness.

No one knows the pain my mind has to bear,

I am smitten by a grief that none can describe.

It comes to roost in the rafters of my broken mind

And has waylaid my peace.

Only God knows my plight.

My thoughts have turned surreal,

Life has become a pathless track:

I want to get away from it for a while

And then come back and all over

For me, life is more a thought than a feeling.

The only way to exorcise the fear

Is to probably laughing at it.

Yes, I have grown remote from pain,

I have spent my life in apocryphal waters.

My world has died

And I write to mourn its unnoticed passing.

18. An Empire Of Darkness

I sit alone

On this measureless night.

Minutes seem to weld into hours,

My eyes fixed on the shadows overhead,

Mouth dry, suddenly puckering

Then the burbling, rumbling from an upset stomach,

A starlit night over the shores of serendipity.

And now, each night I count the stars

As they twinkle interminably from the dark canvas.

And when they will not come to be counted,

I will smear them out of my sight.

Moonlight tosses and turns as before.

I can't bend the firmament of stars:

I decide to cradle them in my eyes,

They seem to be placed in the sky with great precision.

I grope in the grotty little room,

The loneliness stifles the subdued light
That can illumine the hollows of the earth,
I know that I'll fall asleep tonight
But not whether I'll wake up.
Outside the window stretches the sky,
Far off, the blazing thunder bellows her despair.
A bolt of lightning tears open the dark sky
As thunder roars like a famished beast.
The votive Diwali wicks splutter
With their last dregs, dripping away the light.
The night stretches far like an eternity,
Dark like death, the grim reaper.
The interminable waves of
Tears and sleeplessness have gouged into my eyes.
Worries spread their wings on the Milky Way.
Dreams, as solid and dead as night, descend
Like clouds in a murderous rage
Much like loneliness skirting the stream.

A flood of questions keeps tossing around in my head
Amidst the wild chatter of shivering teeth.
My bruised heart murmurs faintly.
The solitary bird of grief sits quietly on the thick branch
Of my haunting loneliness.
The silence is like a large frozen lake
And I am numbed at its shearing edge.
I hope against hope for sleep to embosom me,
Come tender sleep, and soothe my weary eyes.
My sizzling brain continues to tick
Guarding the eyelids from shrouding the eyes.
It can't be sedated even by drugs.
The night has drained away my sleep
From the bowels of the eyes,
The smouldering fires in my bosom
And the live coals in my eyes.
Waiting for somebody to douse them.

The pretty parrot's prattle fails to cheer me.
I stare at the quiet stars in the face for an answer
And the moon appears - but it is no solace.
The silver round host in a cold scythe,
Mercury has sunk in the mouth of a dying day.
The stars spin within their prescribed swings;
My mind was loose and apocalyptic again.
The eyes have grown plum and swollen
With hours of staring and weary longings.
Could somebody blow out the candle?
And allow me to sleep?
Memories keep eluding me,
The treadmill of mind retching my brain,
Reviving the scars of days gone by.
They spawn new tensions like passions
From a shoal of fire-bubbles.
They flock around me
Like scudding hordes of terrorists

And wreck my peace.
I wish I could have thrown them out
For vultures to peck at, to live on.
The blood turns cold like the moon,
I can smell violence in the air
Like the lash of coming rain.
Vast mottled clouds of hatred drifting
Across the placid moon.
I knot myself in the sheets
Muttering fevered curses,
Fighting off the mountains
Flying through the sleep,
My battered heart murmurs silently.
Could somebody soothe my plum eyes
Or embellish my mindscape of despair?
It could blow away the painful insomnia.
My brain aches in the merciless wind
That springs upon the window at eventide.

The stench of burdened, burning air
Keeps me awake, my brain ticking.
The mind is in deep ferment as it lashes fast,
The mutiny rises in the bounds of the skull.
How can I resolve the daily *Kurukshetra*
Of mind, body and soul?
Could somebody put ice on my burning head?
Could somebody pull my eyeshades low?
It can hood the eyes and soothe the turmoil.
Could somebody open the distant door?
It can allow the breeze to walk in.
I suddenly feel somebody walking down
But no, I am wrong.
The heavy feet have grown soft
And Suddenly there is a grim calm
Then a storm rages in the womb of the night.
I have to live through the tortuous hours,
Darkness is its apparel, weirdness is its face.

The candles they have lit in my room
Curse - inverting the deeps of darkness,
The night is a capricious lady,
It stalks like a flaming tyrant
As I struggle to conquer the angel of sleep.
I know I have to endure the passage of night,
The wearier weight of a haunted darkness
When moments shudder from each other.
It appears to be a journey through hell,
Distressing and grieving thoughts creep in
Like frayed shadows of madness
When night comes, dragging its long face,
Dressed in mourning,
But I take solace that the moon too is alone
And night will not get darker after midnight.
Two stars smoothen into my fretted sockets,
Then comes a happy moment
Of which there is no stir in the tree

Nor any portents in the sky.

Till the faint gleam of twilight

Dispels the night's cold gloom

Anal helps me rise above the miasma.

19. The Colour Of Justice

Justice was the salt of every civilization
Its luminescent eyes were folded blind:
Its strong hands were trusted with a sword
That fell on all with equal vigour
Be they of any class, rank or religion.
But what have we done to the virgin lady?
The bandage hides two festering sores
That once perhaps were blindfolded eyes,
Now a tattered patchwork holds the oozing blood.
The hand that held the sword has palsied
And innocence has melted into rancour.
Yes, justice has become ill and senile,
Its commandments have been dehydrated,
No one knows what turns its whims take.
The light of Liberty's beacon has dimmed
Even as one fears the looming doomsday.

Our compass of right and wrong

Has been yanked away and

Our conscience has been leached.

We have ushered in an age of betrayals.

Every prospect of new sunlight

Brings a shadow of embitterment.

Justice itself appears a rusty weighing scale

That will spoil anyone who seeks it.

People change opinions as often as they change clothes.

Truth was the nectar of all cardinal values

But even the flowers have wilted.

God's temple has grown impoverished,

Honour being lost at busy crossroads.

The paradox is that even the greatest truths

Are made to appear the most grotesque lies

In the sparring skills of lawyers.

For those whose hearts still retain a fading light

Truth is no longer a radiant beacon,
It has dug for them their own grave.
The ruining civilization has seeded its spores
In the quagmire of people's marshy souls
Where toxic shoots are sprouting every day.
Freedom is that loving precious gift
For which tears are no recompense
Yet, what has freedom brought to bear?
For those whose body suffers from toil
And those whom hunger stares every hour
What message can freedom ever bring?
It is another corridor to oppression.
Liberty has multiplied the means of coercion
By which the rich fork out wealth
From the wailing bellies of the poor.
Money has gobbled them all,
These brutal fiends, authors of death,
Unleashing primal passions,

Bracing in wait for dragon's breath.

As they sway on the lunatic fringe

They need to unlatch the defiled minds

And let in a fresh breeze of sanity.

It needs surgeons, not bandages.

I see a horizon lit with blood,

An ethical fog closing in on us,

An army of loony, lascivious men on the run,

Merciless men with unanimated hearts.

As I see atavistic passions ruling the world

Darkness has thrown down a challenge

And now the last ray fades.

In this dusk land, only jackals

Have reason to celebrate.

If the salt has lost its savour,

Wherewith shall it be salted?

20. Fantasy

Do you remember the sun-white days?

During our school breaks, we used to sit

Under the huge sage-like banyan tree

Munching sandwiches and teasing crows.

And then we would dream in colourful fantasies

That men are gentle flowers

And all women are silken roses.

And do you remember the long

Milkless midwinter days

As we chattered our way along,

The evenings long as eternity and

Of course the stormy monsoon when

We would navigate our paper boats in the brooks

And pray that the rains will never end,

You remember? I once told our group

That soon there won't be any darkness,

And we could play and be merry all day.
And dusk soon got canopied by darkness,
With a shuddering, we tried to put down
The heavy cup of sleep. And do you remember
Your joy in the middle of the night
When you wake feeling on your head
The touch of a callused palm
And all of us turned into whoops of delight?
Yes, I do remember all those fantasies.
And feel so sheepish about it all.
Now I know that not everyone can see
His dreams come true in the same way.
After seeing the wickedness of Man
I can't believe I was as innocent as I was.

21. For My Late Uncle

How dearly I remember my uncle!

The silence was his costume; smile his language.

Love and compassion were his religion.

He poured them in overflowing streams.

His voice would always ring out a warm welcome.

Inmost in his heart was a sanctuary of love -

Once inside this fabled land

You would stop looking for an exit,

You would be happy to be lost in its labyrinths.

Happiness was as much part of him as his skin.

His magic instilled joy all around.

He would transmute every dull hour into ecstasy,

His avuncular love was a magnetic field

Around which gravitated his nephews and nieces.

He offered breathing space our parents denied,

He was a surrogate parent to so many of us.

His face had taken on a spiritual transparency
Li.ke the glowing serenity of a monk.
The burden he tried to raise
Was too heavy a load, too big a task.
He did raise the heavy crust
But under its weight slept his final sleep.
It was a bond that snapped like a dry twig,
It was all so sudden, I could never reconcile.
The shadow of separation lengthens along
And I tremble if the bond may snap wearily
By the mundane cares of life's draught.
I breathed and walked in his shadow,
I carry him within me wherever I go,
Fragments of him still walk through my mind.
I want to run back through time to uncover
The years that have taken him from me.

22. Vain Thoughts

Why do you mourn the dried flowers?
Tomorrow the garden might turn to weeds.
Why do you feel sorry for today's grief?
The beautiful rose you see in grandeur
Will soon be disarrayed into dust
Like a mush of decayed leaves.
The lovely petunia buds blossom
And then finally shrivel like crumpled paper.
The glistening verdant leaves will freckle with fungus
And welter in the misty dust.
It has to happen with everyone on earth.
So why be rueful about things missed in life?
Be happy with those you have gained,
Don't you see people who have missed even them?
Death and decay are there for each one of us,
Be it the rose, the cypress, the jasmine, the hyacinth,

We came from the loving mother's womb
And we have to go back to the earth's tomb.
Don't you remember our town's millionaire?
He was once the boast and toast of the town.
Yet his death got scant notice among people!
We once saw obeisant crowds beat a retreat to this place
Where now even hungry dogs and beggars don't abound
His shame was all the worst he could wish for,
He lost his haughty, arrogant, sneering pride,
And died as a man before his life slowly ebbed out.
Even people who buzz around you like bees
Are only those who come to suck nectar
And would desert you like the wily insect
That abandons the flowers after draining them.
It is much like the chrysalis which senses
The golden swirl it holds as its form

Will throb to the celestial beat forever
And finds itself dull and hollow
When the throbbing turns
Into a drumming of wings and life flies out.
We all have to come and go unknown
Between the forceps and the tomb.
Over time, you will lose yourself
Although you have not even found yourself yet
A tiredness overcomes you and your soul,
It finally verges on the rejection of life itself.
You could have found an open-door
But you could not have run away from your burden
The helplessness was in yourself.
Everything passes. Everything falls.
An untainted heart is more precious than
All the filthy lucre in the world.

23. Subterfuge

Your sight sends shivers up my spine.

Your face has no coarseness

And your eyes have gentle pupils

But still, your sight sends shivers to me.

It is not your face, your eyes, or your voice,

It is your conceited mind, deceitful actions

And your cleverly hooded mischief

Which have bedevilled my peace

And made me lose faith in Man.

You don't speak any harsh language:

You don't even frown at me.

At times, you even use sweet words

And conceal your pride under a meek and poker face

But these are all counterfeit actions.

Your real you is much unlike you,

You wear so many masks,

Perhaps you are the swiftest turncoat.
What to say of your rapid somersaults,
The quick-cawed dart of your eyes
Is a wild thorn in my serene flesh?
Your gentle eyes conceal a devil's mind,
You are a devil in man's cloak.
At least Satan is Satan for me,
But you are a cruel imposter:
Sometimes an angelic face, saintly eyes,
But always a Satan dwelling in you.
Your soul is the soul of a hawk.
Our acquaintance is good only for narcissistic dignity.
I know I was a willing cadge to your plans,
I burnt my fingers, my reputation, and my soul.
You feel your chameleonic mischiefs are clandestine
And remain furtive from my gentle eyes
But beware, a day will certainly come
When your actions will chain you

And ever-sharpening human claws
Will tear your filthy charities apart.
Your wolfish acts and charlatanry
Will burn your deeds in a cruel flame.
The redeeming hand of Providence
Will humble your devilish head.
Morality is not a slippery eel that can
Assume any shape and wiggle past anything.
I have now seen through your subterfuge.
Yes, you are a pathological hypocrite.
People will bring you down on your knees
And drop you like a hot potato.
Their revenge will filigree your hair like light
And the freight for the bad karma
Will stash your burgeoning wealth.
You will get your just desserts
But you can still shrug off the oncoming tragedy
By doing deeds in expiation,

It is never too late

To repent and reform.

There's an ocean of mercy

In the house of the Lord.

24. False Gods

They hungrily sniff for gullible men

To plant and grow their raw passions.

Huge sums of money

Are scooped up as subscriptions

From the toiling petty labour

To foot the astronomical expenses

Of these self-styled gods.

The bankrupt slogans are throated

Down gullible throats

And laws transgressed by the poor

To feed the hungry pride of the leaders

Which is bigger than their shadows.

The wannabe leaders

Goad people to face bullets

And then use death as pawns for selfish ends.

The faithful died for a cause -

Distilled from the leader's mad frenzy,
The leader's goal is what they sought.
But the martyr's blood has flown in vain,
It was meant to soothe the egos of these vampires
Who keep spewing the lava of mistrust.
The slain is soon forgotten -
No sirens are sung, no bugle sounded,
Not even his name grafted on stone,
Not even a customary obituary, no memorial, no tomb,
Not even a medal or insignia to adorn the shelf,
His wife bawling for bread,
The leaders still extorting benefits
From the state and police.
These sanctimonious windbags,
Their rhetoric dancing on the blood of the slain,
Have few qualms about these actions,
Hypocritically clad in homespun,

Cooped in their air-conditioned homes,
Fuelled by their obsequious buddies and lackeys
Who lionise them as dazzling heroes.
The people's plight can hardly rouse
The scarlet pulsing in their veins.
Even prayers are part of hypocrisy's tools.
These are the new-breed leaders,
Their black and wicked souls
Remain supine to mundane injustices
That their tongues have begun to rot.
A cupid avarice burns in their hearts.
They deliver loud harangues on morality and ethics
And dole out character testimonials.
This is the real face of our leaders,
The harbingers of so many tomorrows.

25. Nouveau Riche

Here under tottering shacks

Kids quarrel over soggy rice.

In front stands the regal tower

Echoing mirth and extravagance.

Ensconced on sandalwood sofas

Holding silver forks and amber tumblers

Slicing grilled meat and holding champagne

Greedily sucking the sweat of the poor

These wealthy overweening gadabouts

Live in a mythical time

And scorn at poverty - grim and stark.

They talk glibly of socialism while

Enormous amount of money is swilling around

In the fishbowl of their social circuits

Dancing in a macabre ritual of social peacockery.

They slouch around with a brogue in vogue

Their pockets jingling with gold coins,

But in their hearts, avarice has no bounds

Driving in limousine comfort, their totems of affluence

Living life in flamboyant auto-pilot mode,

They roll up the windows sealing themselves tight,

Shutting out the beseeching beggars,

Courting rich bars for premium champagnes.

When they happen to stumble upon the poor

Abuses come gushing out of their gaping mouths,

They use the foulest language with the vilest behaviour.

Can there be no digression from superhighways

To the squalid path, foodless tables, roofless homes?

Children look pale and sick like tender banana leaves,

Death notices drop thick and fast on poor dwellings.

Here is all grief - only hotels, and banquets spouting joy.

Nothing can melt the stony hearts of our elite.

What the eye does not see

The heart does not grieve about,

Their sparrow brains

Ringing like jingles in their skulls,

The old man hobbling, coughing and wheezing.

These self-proclaimed deliverers of humanity,

When they start losing wads of currency notes,

They fumble in their pockets scrounging the last pence

For the last ounce of champagne

And then they stagger back homeward

Blaming it all to a sad star.

All this under the cold eye of the creator.

Colossal oppression masquerades

In the robes of democracy

And with iron feet, it tramples down

The weak without remorse.

One nation pastures on the other
One sows the grain that another harvests.
Philosophy teaches that bread is to
Be pilfered from the hands of the weak
And his soul was sent from his body.
Extortion of one's fellowmen
Is the law of the new civilization?
And it conceals itself
Behind the veils of commerce.
Give the rich respect and glory as their prize,
Fob off the poor with promises of paradise.
This human fodder may burst into balefire –
For every swank mall that springs up in a booming city
A neglected debt-ridden village will explode in rage.

26. The Tinctured Heart

He was a wounded man
Unable to be cured by herbs.
He was bitten by a man,
His wound was beyond surgeons.
It woke him from deep slumbers
Burning the mind with its cinders,
It drove him to haunted asylums
Where acrobatics of fellow inmates bewildered him
And he found himself in ghostly aprons
Sucking barbiturates, staring at prison walls.
This reek of madness would keep returning to him.
Some said he was under a spirit
And took him to a soothsayer.
They went to shamans and mystics
Then to the local baba's exorcising assembly
The baba chanted beaded formulae

And the crowd parroted it sotto voce.
With every word, dozens of hands came crashing together
Clapping in unison, in perfect chime with the beat
As the babbling chant grew into a crescendo,
Undulating and soaring over the bungalow.
The baba's blazing protuberant jinn-like eyes
And hooked nose sat on a rugged face that
Forested a haystack of raffishly hennaed beard,
The swarthy forehead was smeared with dollops of ash.

The hectoring tone made him
Look like the younger brother of a brown Jehovah.
A shimmering green satin
Draped his well-fed portentous frame.
Spittle flecked his betel-reddened lips
As if they were bleeding.

He would keep blowing red saliva.
A pair of monstrous whiskers
Jutted arrogantly out of his face
Giving a burlesque ugliness to his ravenous head,
The sharp minatory glance of his eyes
Raging in a violent gaze.
Like a hawk, he darted his eyes on women who
Swarmed the room like flies
Snorting and wailing,
Buzzing the names of God a hundred times
As their shrill chants rose up
With the smoke and redolence
From the smouldering embers of scented coal.
Then begins the Baba's voodoo with his bands,
Hysterical women banging their heads and braids
And rolling their bodies with paranoid frenzy,
Their famished bodies an easy sport for the devils
The cascading hair brooming the floor,

The quivering lashes, the ruddy eyes

Swaying to the rhythmic dance,

The soul forgets its suffering

As it glides into pleasure.

The baba chanting doggerels. his broom-like shaggy mane

Caressing the closing circle of women,

He blew the sacramental mantra in their ears.

His anger flowed like lava out of a volcano

As he kept flagellating the poor man

As the horrified woman cringed in fear

Aghast, bedazzled and transfixed in thought

At the sight of the sinewy, tribal shuddering,

Writhing and squirming on the ground.

Yet no sign of the ghost being scorched.

The baba frowned in disgust.

The open flame licked at the tasselled

Edges of the peacock feather,

Slowly indigo, emerald, gold, bronze,
The whole shimmering spectrum of colour
Was reduced to ash which consecrated the room.
The baba dusted the powder
And daubed the head with emetic pastes.
Then began a strange flow of chants:
Half songs, half-spoken verses,
Words that locked into each other
As tightly as bones in a hand.

Faster and faster went the chanters,
Faster and faster flew the words.
Amidst the loud peels of scruffy clairvoyants
The baba then flogged the spirit!
He wrestled the man into a headlock.
The baba was a corpulent figure and the slim
A man bent as easily as a dog's tail in his grip.
"Come on you swine, you defiler of humans"

The baba hollered angrily.
The rhythm pounded through the women's bodies
As they sat timorously kissing their amulets.
It is gone; "I have paralyzed the evil one,"
The baba proudly boomed in his baritone voice,
And the man lay squirming like a writhing infant,
Still the same wreck he was.
The baba was a charlatan
Reaping the harvest of ignoramuses.
The patient was a wounded man
Unable to be cured by herbs.
He was a man bitten by a man.

27. Friendship

Why do you want to change me?

Accept me as I am.

Don't you feel everyone has a right to live

According to his lights -

Am I not a being with a mind, a heart

And a soul of my own?

I would like to be guided by my lights

Even if they may not be as clarified as yours,

But they are my very own,

My long trusted lights.

Don't love me for my smile.

Don't love me for my eyes.

A love like that will never survive.

Would you love me if I could never smile again?

Would you love me if I lost my sight?

Let's ride the waves and troughs

For we are friends beyond compare,

We have sutured our relations stitch by stitch.

Did I ever ask you to change?

I could have if I lacked sincerity,

But I honestly felt,

Why should I prevent you

From living your happy way?

I have lovingly accepted you as you are

And my humble request is:

Accept me as I am.

All I want is to be loved

And to be accepted for the imperfect being that I am

That is the most natural way

Of manuring our friendship.

I have no gentle words

To heal your pain

No tender look, nor touch -

Only my pain in yours searing the raw edges of a bond.

Accept this, if you will,

Then let's part, though not in anger,

And restore each to the other

A chastened self, but not defeated.

Love me for the love I return,

This love will never die.

It will live well beyond the realms of time.

I'll return the precious love you gave me.

You and I hold many secrets,

Closely concealed stories of sorrow

Neither of us would dare to tell,

Rather live in silence to protect each other.

Nobody needs to know the truth,

It would scare and scar their hearts.

Nevermore should we live in silence,

Holding heavy our burdens alone.

Together always seemed but a dream,

For you and me that dream is true.

I will meet you again

How and where I know not

To pour out the last remnants of discontent.

My secrets cling to you

Because your hemisphere completes

The fractured circle of my history.

Before the evening deepens into night

Let me write the last secret

Before night refolds and screens us away,

Although we've already dived into the ocean

Of each other's souls

From the wilderness of your heart.

Time does not end here. Let us moan no more

From what depths

Well up even these smiles of ours!

I am but a pinch of dust just a little nobler than a sod;

I am but an ember wrapped in a frame wrung out of clay;

Let us work out our salvation with diligence.

Not farewell, but fare forward, dear voyager.

28. Without Ceremony

He was twenty.

It was broad daylight

As savage men

Slaughtered him

Like a festival goat

Even as a hundred etherised humans

With plastic eyes and

Clay tongues

Stood passive and mute,

Not even a word uttered as the grisly macabre dance

Was over in the wink of an eye.

The pale figure was led forth

And bound to a post.

There was not even a death rattle.

The cold fat black crows stood still

Uncaring, watched by an indifferent sun.

Even as the serried sheep
Scampered away into safe bushes,
The hollow men, the stuffed men
Stood as speechless shadows
Like a herd of mortified lambs
With not a single moan of protest.
The wind moved across their sphinx faces
Like the fingers of an archaeologist.
I ask these hundred statues not out of sorrow,
But in wonder,
Why did you turn away to belong to
A sly and treacherous world?
I never knew you had feet of clay.
A phalanx of shrouded women
Stepped out from
An overlooking lane
Swatting a wreath of flies
And laid out

A white sheet

On the corpse.

As the corpse lay impaled,

Pyred on the hard earth,

The caped body still letting out blood,

Surrounded by the stench of carrion

The women appeared nightly among

The squawks of mynahs and

The flapping of crows

As a wheeling vulture scanned the field.

He was twenty.

It was broad daylight

As savage men

Slaughtered him

Like a festival goat.

The wind of rebellion

Attacked land and sky.

The corpse had carved a logo, a philosophy.

Voices ceased to be heard.

Time stopped and held its breath.

The heaving land groaned around.

The women wailed hysterically.

The world looked at them, closed its eyes

And walked on, rubbing its hands.

Yet, somehow I know

The birds that herald dreams

Were exiled from their song,

Each voice was torn out of its throat.

They dropped into the dust

Even before the hunter strung his bow.

Oh, God! Bless these impaled bodies

With the passion for your resurrection;

Make their dead veins flow with blood again

The miracle of the world

Will be wrought again.

The space will be filled

Despite the hurt

By the immensity of love.

Truth shall spring out of the earth,

Justice shall pour down from the heavens.

29. Separation

The sunset has brought us together.

We have a night to spend

Under the shadow of thoughts,

But a silence to endure.

Silence between us

Is like a thread to hold

Under the shadow of darkness.

Stray thoughts perch

On softened lips

And crinkles sit

On the tightness of cheeks.

The sunrise will soon

Drive us apart,

Each to his world.

So, why not divulge

The secrets of hidden affairs?

30. Reprieve

There is a clash of arms

In the distant corners

Of my forbidden city.

Men in furious rage

Pillage innocent houses

Like hungry dogs

And voracious wolves

On a foraging spree.

A rapacious and abominable lot

In a wild and murderous rage

Running amok with maces, tridents and cleavers

Like a comet's tail of violence.

Sundered hands and feet strewn around

I can hear the rattle of death

Violence walks along the streets, smilingly not naked.

The mangled and manacled are dragged

To the shameless cheers of these human hounds

And there isn't a scream in the dark sky

The last bus is leaving the town,

The eyes still looking for a reason to board it.

31. The Brute

They do not have any trace
Of human semblance,
These are the two-legged brutes.
The smouldering flame
Flares in a cumulus
From maelstrom depths,
While here in my abode
I grope in the dark
Rustling promiscuous heaps.
The cluttered files
Display the clan's life.
But here lay the tribe
Slaughterecl and exterminated.
From the low embers rise shrill cries
Resonating with the funeral dirge
Of a short-lived clan.

32. Farewell To A Friend

The limpid waters of the river
Rustle along the shores
Until the heavy rocks block their way.
I bid farewell to my friend.
A demure young lad he was:
His mind was as clear as a computer,
His convictions are tough as a rock.
The night has already begun
To spread its looming canopy.
The time is now to rise and speaking
Out our love. Your ideas broke the mould
Of prejudice in which my mind was formed.
You let the world in on my weak shoulders.
We hemmed and hawed over ideas held in common.
The moment of separation has now come.
The line of the horizon has started fading,

He walks to the north and I to the south.

His faint memories, like floating clouds,

Shall always populate my universe.

A shadow falls on us and grows.

Tomorrow we will meet, again at a different latitude.

We embrace in the haze of sunset

And part with eyes bloated

And hearts bulging with the pain of separation.

33. The Cleanest Creation

I search hard for the cleanest creation
Of the omnipotent Lord.
The fragrance of the lovely enchanting rose
Cleans my heart of its dross
And embellishes my desiccated mind.
Our bodies are mere husks of flesh and bone.
The beautiful butterfly
And the glistening soothing leaves
Whose chlorophyll will get syringed out
Will soon turn to carcasses and rotting debris;
The orchards will vanish, the gardens will wither,
The crops will wilt, the verdure will turn hay,
Arise, ripen, decay and never return.
You know how autumn makes a ghost of the trees:
It strips them bare to the skin,
It shakes out their hearts, the green out of leaves,

Then what is the cleanest creation?

The perfect miracle may be found only in man:

Vast stretches of whiteness

That radiate truthfully.

The cleanest thing is not the twilight

Nor was the sky reflected in the river, nor

The sun on apple blossoms.

All these are finally lowered to their burial.

It is love - the love that is as sparkling white

As the new-born lily,

As clean and clear as a child's tear.

The love that gives new life

To a wilting heart.

The love whose glow is strong enough

To dispel the gloom of darkness.

34. Lessons Of Saintliness

Where has saintliness led him?

To keep him an angel, his wife

Carted her peace and health

To the neighbourhood.

Mortgaged dwelling and groaning debts,

Dignity pledged to the sahukar,

Bank balances moving in a red curve,

This is the harvest of his foolish benevolence,

Suffering for self; gratification for others:

These were the testimonials

But, what now?

No money for even a soggy half-meal:

Wife and kids being cruelly thrashed,

Tyrannical creditors thronging the door,

The wily neighbour has bolted his door.

What now?

The dutiful wife removes her bangles,

Watch, pendant, the wedding ring.

The cruel creditors need to be silenced,

The fire of the belly to be sublimated

And the mind soothed back to reason.

What has happened to your saintly ideas?

Clean thoughts and noble deeds,

They remain dark vain principles.

The revolution was too short-lived,

The heart has grown

The words still ringing in his heart

But the song has lost its music.

There is nothing to salvage; now all is lost

As you keep dodging people to

Keep up failed promises. Charity must begin at home!

35. The Real Face

You will never know his natural face.

He smiles, and you consider him happy.

Behind his invented face is the natural face.

Do you want to see his natural face?

Then see the heavy wrinkles and fissures

Which life's pains have dug into his face?

The bottled tears have furrowed his cheeks,

He has grown stubble on his chin.

You unsleeved his spotless clean shirt

And you will find ageing, aching veins,

A skin that is as brittle and closely veined as

A dried eucalyptus leaf.

The veins stand out like the outlines of bare trees,

The plaque veins in which flows sluggishly

The blood flared at the sight of injustice.

He invented a face for himself.

Behind it, he lived, died and resurrected
So many times in his life.
His face has wrinkles of that face,
His wrinkles have no look,
He will never show his natural face.
It was the silent revolution that he had won
Against the mad darkness. So believing,
My life grew meaningful, and where before
I felt myself an atom in the void
I am now engaged to join other men
To keep the light alive and especially
To oppose all those who would re-enthrone
The darkness and betrayal. In the name of light
This they have nearly done.
And I, in the prime of life, have felt
The anguished bitterness that exiles know.

36. Ritual

He lights the joss sticks.
And fans them across the
Assortment of divinities
That wrestle for a place
In his crowded shop.
Then he burns the incense to them all.
He kisses the plastic murals.
In a thirty-minute ritual
Performed daily
With the precision of a priest.
Then begins his trade,
Robbing fifty grams on every kilo
And passing off fakes as originals
And adulterated as pure
Under the eloquent testimony
Of the glowing saints.

A sooty visage of Gandhi,
A pantheon of celluloid gods and goddesses,
Almond-eyed and swollen-breasted,
Beckon at us from every niche.
The poor folks are happy.
At getting groceries on credit.
And they don't mind paying debts.
Cleverly rounded off to higher digits
By his sleigh-of-hand accounting.
In all this drama
The divinities keep smiling
As he keeps placating the deities
Amidst the glow of incense and joss sticks.

37. Compassion

He comes home without a penny.
Like so many days in the month
When the contractor sends him back.
He comes back home at the same time,
Whether it is work or no work.
But his wife can read it well:
Glum face, crooked gait, and sullen eyes
As he staggers back with a melancholy look.
Had it not been for the saintly wife
He may have never returned.
She ushers him with soothing words:
"Lord is great. He has brought you back."
She offers a tumbler of water and tea,
Shame has filled the belly full, and
There is no desire for even soggy rice.
Fortunately, children have cried to sleep.

She has still not lit the fire, and

The vessels stand cleanly washed.

But something must still be there.

She picks a dirty vessel, scrubs it hard,

She scrapes it till her nails hit the metal

And then slips the morsel into his mouth

It has the flavour of a wife's love,

His face lights up.

The woman is the only creature.

Who can fit herself into any mould?

She has the malleability that makes
her adapt

To any relationship.

The woman is the only creature.

Who can fit herself into any mould?

A woman is rarely a seducer, always a nourisher,

She is always a great mind expert and a
soul healer,

She knows how to calibre emotions into gentle cadences.

In her lie, nature's best qualities of motherhood,

She has natural traits that men can never fathom.

38. Freedom

I want to be free,

I want to be me.

Why do people want to heap advice on me?

Why do they want to poach on my privacy?

They may be my friends.

Or could be my enemies:

But why do they want to seize

My right to live my way?

Sometimes I feel

As if I am forever a child

Looking at life and asking many "whys",

Never understanding the complexity

Of the world led by adults. Feeling overwhelmed

By the rules and restrictions that so many seem to enforce

Trying to overpower my life

As if I am forever a child

In need of a guardian. I want to be free,

I want to be me. My lights are my lights,

They may not burn brightly.

But they are my own,

My very own authentic lights,

And they know well which way to light up my path.

My voice is my voice,

It knows what to speak.

My conscience is my compass:

It knows where to point the needle.

I want to be free,

I want to be me.

I know what is good for me,

I know what is bad for me.

Why do you want to intrude into my peaceful world'?

I'm the light of no man's eye,

The rest and solace of no man's heart am I,

Just a handful of dust, am I,

Let me live the way I am,

Let me be free,

Let me be me.

39. The Sleepless Night

During the whole night
Everybody snored in blissful rhythms;
But I struggled on a parched bed,
As I shuffled restlessly,
Gripping the chilly rails of the bed,
My eyes were driven into hollow sockets.
Weirdness enveloped the night's skull.
The warm blood and the frazzled brain
Dispelled the scalloped clouds of sleep
Which limped slowly into the cerebrum.
My heart started beating madly.
I counted the stars in the sky
And computed them with my capaciousness.
The moon, too, appeared to be sad and lonely.
My eyes clamoured for a pulse of respite
But my thimble-edged fingers picked

The sprouting seeds of adversity
From the soil of burnished memories.
The departed years hark at me,
Vivid memories get dredged up
From the depths of my mind.
They keep screening wild across my eyes,
It was an atmosphere of febrile confusion.
A chilling fear consumed me,
The daffodils of my bloomed hair
Shrivelled away under the drought
That stalked my scalp. The dry cranium
It wouldn't allow green shoots to grow greener.
Myths nestle in my cobwebbed mind.
They hibernate, imprisoned by time,
And churn out nightmarish dreams
Congregating countlessly all around.
Delirious dreams rage
Like a fever in the blood.

The night slowly wanes into the wilderness
Till twilight emerges
From the ashes of darkness.
Waking up is a parachute jump from nightmares
Marred by the suffocating tempest.
A new day rescues me from the painful night.
I feel as if I am an inmate of a prison
Who's just got out on parole,
Dreadfiil of being driven back to confinement.

40. Friendship

Our friendship should not be taken for granted.

We have to water it with the sweat of love,

The emotions are yet to solidify and thicken.

The bond is still not tenacious enough

To withstand the rough and tumble of life.

Our daily pleasantries may go smooth

But the real test is when grief strikes us

Or when friendship entails a loss or sacrifice.

Be it money, self-esteem, or career,

If the bond that has brought us close

It is the bond of selfishness. It is as fragile as a dry twig,

It is going to snap any moment.

It will remain a tower built on quicksand

And will crumble under the mildest quake.

Such a friendship can't jell,

It will only be a symbiotic bond.

Friendship ought to be a companionship of souls,

Each bristling with honest affection

True friendship requires the effacement of self.

Let it not be stained with selfish thoughts,

Let us respect each other's lives,

Let it not be couched in a coat of ambiguity.

If we keep judging each other

We will have no time to love.

Friendship must have the clarity of a
shepherd's flute.

Let us accept our follies without judgment

And look for no proof of the bond.

You must realize that two men.

Can look at the same thing and see it
differently

Because feelings, if worded, lose their flame.

I have no gentle words to heal your pain,

No tender look nor touch. Only my pain in yours

Searing the raw edges of a bond

Yet holds and will not break.

So accept me with all my flaws

And I will do the same.

41. A Failed Saint

No, you have failed!
You feel you are a saint,
A paragon of perfect virtue.
Your wife has burnt her dreams
And your blooming children
Have wilted into psychic souls,
Your house is still the two-room
Dingy tenement
With the stench of moisture.
The curtains are crying for a wash
And the sofa creaking for repairs
But do you know
Your benefactors are now living
In opulent mansions with nylon curtains,
Regal sofas and the scent of roses?
Your woolly idealism

Has driven you away

From the hard realities

Of life at home.

Your generosity made you no rich man,

Nor too much kindness a healer of heartbreaks

After the evenings that drained the life out of you.

You are out of sleep when you need it most.

42. Endurance

Thirty scorching days

Of fasting

To endure. T

But she does it dourly;

My young sister wakes up

To the muezzin's sonorous call.

She gulps

White loaves of bread,

Munching them

With glistening teeth.

The day moves like an ant

And she fades

Into a hungry girl,

Counting minutes for the muezzin's call

To break the long ordeal.

The face has grown weary

But eyes have become
More expressive.
The body has been drained.
Of the material dross.
But the mind has lit.
With a spiritual glow.
For a small girl
It is a harrowing ordeal.
She remains the chirpiest folk.
In our family
And when last night I tiptoed up
To her room and heard her
Talking to someone and opened
The door, there was no one there.
Only she is on her knees, peeking into
Her own clasped hands.
The smooth passage
Shows the Maker's impression.

43. Darkness

When I was a child
My mother warned me
Not to cross the darkness.
A horrible bridge spans a devilish sea,
Impish creatures, ghosts and ghouls
Creeping from dark shadows
And haunting the lanes, she said.
I didn't follow the advice
And made forays
Into the hidden universe.
She would clutch my hand and whisper,
In this life, my darling, there is no mercy.
The doting mother
She still won't budge from her words
But the sane father
Would insulate me

From hoary superstitions.

One shows blind love,

The other does not lack it;

His passion has a marrow of reason.

44. Silence

There stretches an eerie silence.

In the valley that separates us.

Don't place the wreaths.

On the empty tomb that shelters, not a soul

But a ghost. There is a vacuum

In the thin air

That blows through the lane,

And a mute silence

That walks on the toes

Of a fruitless warrior.

Don't place the wreaths.

On the empty tomb.

45. Across The Sea

The waves speak in innocence.

But voices wail across the shores.

I am a mute soldier.

On a crestfallen path.

The small tides smile.

In hatred, while the foams

Bulge into a stream of tears.

I must rescue the waters.

For a tornado to pace across the surface,

The moon's image

Contracts into my eyeballs.

But I can't return home

For I have to answer

Voices across the shores.

Darkness floods out the last of an orchid sky.

The house fills up once again.

With the din of whimpering footfalls.

Tonight someone will drink.

The poison of dreams and die once again.

I wait for the stars to reappear

And the moon to disclose her silver horn.

46. Deception

How long can you invent faces?
Some day you show up as a friend
With a gentle smile, a loving heart,
Another day as a troubled man
In need of money and assistance.
I dole out a few hundred rupees
Out of my hard-earned salary,
Then suddenly, I find you in richness,
On a mad, reckless splurge
Entertaining friends
And sloshing at bars.
These acts break compassionate hearts.
And make a man lose faith in man.

47. Time

How fast time rattles across age.

Yesterday I was a child.

Playing with twigs and stones

And plucking berries and flowers

Under the fiery eyes of the landlord.

When he trained his rifle

We would flee at a satanic pace.

Today when I found my son

Rushing into the house

With a handful of berries,

Dusty clothes, fluttering breath

And a face agog with triumph,

I feel he is me.

I remember myself as a boy with athletic feet

Rushing pell-mell to meet life's challenges.

Now time has slowed in the heart;

Through this struggle and strife, I cry in my sleep,
"I have worn away this precious life."
It is the same story.
Scripting and moving the same way.
I can't believe it is thirty years
Since the same acts unfolded throughout my life.
I remember holding a hand, and he'd dawdle,
The pull now hustles him forward
Of something far more potent than school.
They don't appear to be memories
But events that refolded yesterday
As I see the unbridled excitement
That keeps gushing through my son's veins.
Time has run its full circle.

48. Adventure

I came hunkering down the rancid lanes
With sharpened hooks and chiselled twigs
But your eyes twitched with horror
And your limbs crinkled with dry air.
You chunked behind the granite marble
While I eddied in debauched manners
In the remote corridors of boulevards.
Your eyes glistened with fused moisture,
And your hair besmirched into an ugly mess,
As I advanced through scented heliotropes.
My hands were scarred with bloodstains
Till I returned to my parched bed.
The bugs hummed along the plastic walls,
While the heliotropes bowed with courtesy.
You remained ignorant of the mystery
With a hideous tranquillity entrapping you.

The fluid saliva slimed from my mouth

Like the glutinous milk of poppies,

And the dry hair jumbled around,

As unruly as my life

Till the night dried

Into a drought of despair.

49. My Grandma's Tales

Those were days

Of childhood,

When my grandma

Delighted us with tales, anecdotes and fables,

Her face wrinkled as a walnut

And her corrugated forehead

Exuding a saintly aura.

She would wrap our daily dose of scriptures

In lovingly delivered parables.

Her bedtime stories would be cooked with

An assorted variety of characters.

She would cycle ancient wisdom into folklore

And turn out fantastic and succulent fables

From her melting pot

To which she would keep adding new elements

Sometimes she would get so excited that

Her arms would flail and flutter

Like the motors of a distressed helicopter.

That was many sad years ago.

I am now past my golden anniversary,

Neither is there the Superman

Nor somebody from David's tribe

I want to hark back to it.

All I have is this photo.

My grandma's wizened face

Framed in a mop of grey curls

Peering through the gilded case

Exuding a saintly innocence.

My only memories of grandma

In the centre room of our ancestral house

Narrating parables and making tiny pyramidical paans

Out of betel leaves with her knobbly fingers -

Her chewing had a grammar of her own

As we nannies watched her ruminate

While the whole house slept like a beaten army.

50. An Uncertain Leveller

What an uncertain leveller
Death is!
His image stands before me.
In the flesh, blood and clothes.
The same searching eyes.
The same excitement.
The same eagerness.
I brood over the sad news.
How could he die?
How can I believe it?
I have not seen it.
The closed eyes, immobile lips,
Pulseless heart, clenched teeth.
He still smiles at me
And my heart still glows
With the warmth of his fire.

51. The False Dervish

Have you been to any dargah?
I am sure you must have
Been awed
By the make-believe diviners in satin robes
Swaying peacock feathers
And eyeing your pockets,
Their eyes dripping loads of avarice.
The saint buried in this sooty, grimy tomb
Waiting for a genuine devotee to clear the air,
While in the open streets
Priests haggle with terrified devotees,
Selling holy blessings
And immaculate promises
At bargain prices.
The saint would have
He snuffed them with his mystic frown.

Now they swarm around him.

Like barnacles sucking money

From gullible disciples

Under his beatific shadow.

52. Tomorrow

It is the same story today.

Dressed in the same mournful face of

The many yesterdays gone by.

There remains a wish.

That tomorrow may never repeat -

They have endured their hard life.

But what of the crying, hungry baby?

So many tomorrows to go

And so many hungry nights to endure.

When the baby is fast asleep,

It is perhaps the only time

They are spared the pain of her cries.

There is no sleep for them with

Their bellies were belching with hunger.

There is no dream for them

For sleep can't grow deep enough

As to allow a play of phantasies.

She caresses the sleeping baby

And he looks back with tears.

It is the only way they can shower love.

53. Child Labour

The wick of childhood has been drained
Of the glow of innocence.
The flame of adulthood is in its total luminescence
As the tropical heat blanches and sears the tender skin.
For every child who takes wings to study abroad
There will be ten who fall off the map,
Without the raft of a basic alphabet to keep them afloat
These tiny adults have become surrogate husbands
For their sick, abandoned mothers.
Years of mind-numbing toil
They have palsied their power to dream.

54. Death Ward

I handed over my sister the one-size-fits-all
Coarse hospital apron.
She suddenly drooped, looking like
A raft on a stranded island
Devoid of her graceful salwar kameez.
A series of operations had trapped her
In a web of spindly tubes and wires.
The nurse strides out of the ward,
I paced impatiently back and forth
As we wait for the dreadful news.
It can be any moment now.
My heart starts pounding.
At the sight of the grim nurse is emerging.
Is it to convey her informal medical bulletin?
It has been the same story every day
Like this for more than a week.

My sister is in a coma and
Her system was kept alive on a ventilator.
The intravenous drip mutters and splutters,
Syringes being poked now and then,
A pigeon impatiently paced on the sill,
The sparrows fighting for crumbs,
Her innards bulged with toxic fluids.
My mother has been more sensible.
She has been reading the rosary.
Almost round the clock for the final hour.
My sister lost her kidneys l;ong ago,
She survived all these years on steroids
And a borrowed kidney.
My mother became a full-time nurse.
And my father, a part-time counsellor.
They abandoned their personal lives for her.
The ICU was her last home:

White room, white curtains, white-clothed nurses in their

Long white socks cracking white jokes

And scurrying about like smiling white cats.

The doctors made us pour money like water -

The merciless tribe who knew she wouldn't live anymore.

I always considered them the most authentic messiahs.

My experience has painted them as dealers of death.

Looking into my sister's eyes, I read the grim spectacle

That was unrolling in her hazy mind

As she lay swaddled in bone-white gauze,

Beneath the innocence of morning flesh

Slivers of pain shoot in sharp bouts,

Hinting at death, she did not heed.

My father sat in a contemplative mood

Wondering where our relatives and friends had vanished.

A few of them would spasmodically turn up as a ritual

Lest their sincerity be put on trial.

My sister came here for a routine checkup

We took her back as a corpse.

Tears refused to flow out of my mother's eyes.

Embedded deep down in her psyche

It was a rich seam of emotional values.

I watched that serene stone-faced silence.

As I held the caped body, Father signed

The delivery register at the mortuary

After the body was swabbed and embalmed.

I was amazed by my mother's calm as she

Untied the knot at the head to reconfirm it was her daughter.

I shuddered as a thought blazed through my mind:

What if there was a mix-up of corpses

In the rush and commotion of delivering them.

Looking at the cold-hearted insouciance of the mortuary keeper

I felt how my mother's radars blipped at that moment.

My sister quietly went away,

Her final goodbye to the death ward.

Her eyes have frozen in my memory.

We lost her, but she left behind

A vast reservoir of wisdom.

She closed her eyes, yet she opened ours,

She helped us understand people.

55. The Open Door

Everywhere, in every direction, men are running amok.

Bent and bowed by the burden of life,

Man has become a beast of burden,

From dawn to dusk, running like a mad, hysterical being.

No one knows when the night ends or the day emerges,

Every man has become a tomb to his corpse:

No time to think, no time to reason, no time to dream,

Sheeted corpses, clogged streets, squadrons of babus,

The unceasing roar of traffic moving like a snarl,

Hawkers hawking their wares in cockerel voices,

Snorting and wailing amid coughing fits,

Flattened noses and wheezing lungs,

The hands being smelted into lumps

Emitting a rattle of death and decay,

The groan of labourers heaving huge loads
With backs hunched beyond their years,
The whiny drone of the narrator peddling miraculous cures,
The choking, retching, moaning of the starved and hungry.

The dissonant two-tone siren parted the traffic like a knife,
Endless columns of broken people making their way to nowhere,
Nobody minds if a few toes get stepped on. It's chaos.
You are cribbed when you see the festering innards of the city,
Booze and brothel reek through the rancid bylanes,
A home to sex workers, drug dealers, the daily wage earner,
Like sardines, men crammed in monster toys,
A giant insect is fretting in a seven-foot jar.

The scuffle ensues among the fierce-looking beggars

As a foreigner pulls out his wallet to do small charities.

Soon we have a platoon of rag pickers and beggars

Glueing to him like a burr.

Through the commotion, people move as though they are drugged.

The night roars with the laughter of the clay.

www.ingramcontent.com/pod-product-compliance
Lightning Source LLC
LaVergne TN
LVHW041202150826
845673LV00001B/258

* 9 7 9 8 8 9 1 8 6 5 9 7 6 *